Oscar

Oscar

THE LIFE AND MUSIC OF **OSCAR PETERSON**

Reva Marin

GROUNDWOOD BOOKS
HOUSE OF ANANSI PRESS
TORONTO
BERKELEY

Groundwood Books / House of Anansi Press
110 Spadina Avenue, Suite 801, Toronto, Ontario M5V 2K4
or c/o Publishers Group West
1700 Fourth Street, Berkeley, CA 94710

We acknowledge for their financial support of our publishing program the Canada
Council for the Arts, the Government of Canada through the Book Publishing
Industry Development Program (BPIDP) and the Ontario Arts Council.

ONTARIO ARTS COUNCIL
CONSEIL DES ARTS DE L'ONTARIO

Library and Archives Canada Cataloguing in Publication
Marin, Reva
Oscar : the life and music of Oscar Peterson / Reva Marin.
Includes bibliographical references, videography, discography and index.
ISBN-13: 978-0-88899-905-4.–ISBN-10: 0-88899-905-4
1. Peterson, Oscar, 1925-2007–Juvenile literature. 2. Pianists–Canada–
Biography–Juvenile literature. 3. Jazz musicians–Canada–Biography–Juvenile
literature. I. Title. II. Title: Life and music of Oscar Peterson.
ML417.P48M337 2008   j786.2'165'092   C2008-901417-0

Cover photograph courtesy of the
Canadian Pacific Railway Archives, Image no. A21392
Design by Michael Solomon
Printed and bound in Canada

To Matthew

CONTENTS

Photographs follow page 64

Introduction

On December 23, 2007, Oscar Peterson died peacefully at his home in Mississauga, Ontario, following a lengthy illness. He was eighty-two years old. Almost immediately tributes began pouring in from his native country, Canada, as well as from around the globe. Musicians and entertainers, politicians and dignitaries, and thousands of Oscar's devoted fans from all walks of life were eager to pay their respects to the man many regarded as one of the best jazz pianists of all time. At a free public tribute to Oscar a few weeks later, 2,000 people gathered to celebrate his life and career.

So what exactly was there about Oscar Peterson that moved people to honor him, in words and in music, in the days and weeks after his death? For some of his fans, there was no question about it. Oscar was simply a wonderful musician, one who set the standards for jazz piano for generations to follow. Others spoke about his generosity toward younger musicians. But for many others, it was Oscar's ability to achieve so much, despite his humble roots, which was most inspiring. This image of Oscar as a role model was perhaps best expressed by

Her Excellency the Right Honourable Michaëlle Jean, Canada's first governor general of Afro-Caribbean heritage. At Oscar's tribute, Jean recalled the hopes of Caribbean immigrants that their children would achieve their goals, just as Oscar Peterson had achieved his.

But long before Oscar became a famous and successful musician, he had discovered another side to life, a side that was cruel and ugly. One day when he was ten years old, he was sitting in class and minding his own business, when one of his classmates hurled a ruler through the air. The teacher, whose back was to the class, turned around and looked directly at Oscar and another boy, the only two black students in the room.

"I'll bet one of the niggers did it," the teacher announced.

For a moment Oscar couldn't believe what he was hearing. His parents, Daniel and Olive Peterson, had raised him to believe that all people were equal, regardless of the color of their skin. They had urged him to have pride in himself, and to treat others with respect. Stand up for what you know is right, they had said to him. What business did his teacher have to accuse him and his classmate of doing something they had not done?

Oscar Peterson was big and strong for his age, and already there was a dignity about him that would remain with him always. There was no way he was just going to sit there and let his teacher's false accusations ring through the classroom.

"You apologize for that!" he shouted, leaping to his feet.

Oscar was about to learn that the world did not always work the way his parents had taught him. Moments later he found himself standing in front of the principal, his punishment for daring to talk back to his teacher.

Oscar learned an important lesson that day. In his life he

would come across many people who would treat him badly just because he was black. Some would talk down to him or accuse him of doing something wrong even though they had no proof. Others would make it clear he was not welcome in their homes or in their businesses.

These experiences hurt Oscar deeply, and in some ways the hurt never went away, even when he grew up to be a famous musician who was loved and respected around the world. But he knew one thing. His teacher and all the other wrong-minded people were not going to keep him from getting somewhere in his life. He listened to the words of his parents and he followed their example. Life was not easy, they told their children, and life was not always fair. But through hard work and determination, the Petersons would make a better life for themselves. They would not surrender to the injustices of society. They would simply have to work a little harder, do a little better than the people around them, so that they would come out on top.

Hard work and determination would take Oscar Peterson from Montreal's poor immigrant neighborhood of St. Henri to the great concert halls of the world. This is his story, a story about one of the greatest musicians Canada has ever produced, and one of the most highly regarded and successful jazz pianists of his time.

Music Is the Key

Daniel Peterson was born in St. Croix in the Virgin Islands. He was a young man at the start of World War One, and he joined the merchant marine and became a skilled sailor. Suddenly his life was filled with adventure and discovery. He traveled far and wide — to South America, England, the United States and Canada.

His duties aboard ship left him with very little free time. Still, there was something he wanted very badly, and he thought long and hard about how he could get it.

Daniel Peterson loved music, and he had always wanted to play the piano. Of course, there were no pianos on the ships. Besides, how could he find time for formal study when he was spending most of his time sailing from place to place? Then, one day when he was in a store, he came across a collapsible organ that could be folded up and carried around like a suitcase. He purchased it with great excitement. Now, even when he was sailing, he could take his instrument with him.

In his free moments, he set about teaching himself to play the organ and learning more about music. Whenever the ship docked, Daniel would go ashore and hunt around in music stores for books about music theory. Even though he never had a teacher, his playing steadily improved. He was also rising in the ranks of the ship's crew. He became bo'sun, the officer in charge of equipment and the duties of the crew.

He was still a young man, but already he was showing a determination for self-improvement that would continue throughout his life. Later on he would demand that his own children apply themselves to learning with the same determination.

At that time many young blacks were leaving the West Indies, where life was very hard. Daniel decided to try his luck in Canada. In 1917 he arrived in Halifax, Nova Scotia, a common destination for many West Indian blacks. While some chose to remain there, many others decided to move farther west. They had heard that they could make a better living in Montreal, working for the railroad. Soon Daniel moved on to Montreal, and within two years he landed a job with the Canadian Pacific Railway as a sleeping-car porter.

Daniel had not been in the city very long when he met a young woman named Kathleen Olivia John. Olive, as she was called, was also from the West Indies, from St. Kitts. Olive's father, Ishmael John, was a school superintendent who had died when Olive was still a young girl. In the West Indies, education was highly prized, but the education of boys was given priority. As a result, Olive and her three sisters had to wait until their brothers finished their schooling. The brothers were sent to university and became pharmacists. Unfortunately, by that time the family's funds had run dry, and the girls were unable to continue their education.

Then, when she was sixteen, Olive John was offered a job as a cook and housekeeper for an English family moving to

Canada. She accompanied the family to Halifax, and every month she managed to put aside some of her earnings to send back to St. Kitts. Then she and her sister, who had also come to Halifax, heard that they could earn more money in Montreal, and they moved there. Olive continued to work as a domestic in Montreal for many years, long after she married Daniel Peterson and was raising her own family.

Today Montreal is a large cosmopolitan city, one of Canada's leading centers of arts and education. It is hardly recognizable as the city where Daniel and Olive settled around 1920 to raise a family. At that time Montreal was a place where people were mostly left to fend for themselves. There was no public health or public sanitation, services that Montrealers now take for granted. The wealthy could afford to pay extra to get what they wanted, but the poor simply had to go without.

Daniel and Olive had moved to a city where more children died at birth than in almost any other city in the world. Many of the poorer residents had no inside plumbing, and there were open sewers that were breeding grounds for disease. Housing was substandard, with often ten to twelve people crowded together in one room. Montreal was so lagging in public health that it was referred to as "the most dangerous city in the civilized world to be born in."

The Petersons lived in the part of Montreal that was home to most of the black residents of the city: the communities of St. Antoine and St. Henri. At that time these communities formed the western boundary of Montreal. An escarpment divided St. Antoine into two parts. The poor of the district — the Irish, English and blacks — lived in the lower section, while the wealthy professionals lived in the upper section. These two areas were known simply as "below the hill" and "above the hill." Many of the poor people below the hill worked as domestics or laborers for the wealthy above the hill.

Immigrants often come to live in a part of a city where the housing is cheaper, and where other immigrants are already living. This was the case in St. Antoine and St. Henri. There was an even more important reason, though, why so many blacks came to live in this part of Montreal.

The area of St. Antoine lay between the Canadian Pacific Railway (CPR) tracks at one end and the Canadian National Railway (CNR) tracks at the other. It was convenient for the railroad workers to live close to where they worked, and so an entire community sprang up around the railroad stations. By the end of the 1920s, there were twelve hundred to three thousand blacks living in Montreal, and of these, ninety percent of the men were working for the railways. Oscar Peterson would later say that he did not remember "any other Negro my dad's age doing anything else."

Daniel's job as a sleeping-car porter was demanding and often demeaning. He was expected to be available at any time of the day or night to attend to the needs of the traveling public. At times he would be addressed in a rude or discourteous way by passengers who saw him simply as a means to their comfort.

Most people who could afford to travel by train were white, and almost all the people serving them were black. This was no accident. Even after slavery came to an official end in the U.S. in 1865, the rail industry continued to use cheap black labor to fill the many positions that were required to run a railroad. To people who had grown up with slavery as a way of life, hiring blacks to do menial work made perfect sense.

By the end of the nineteenth century, the Canadian-owned rail companies — the CNR and the CPR — were copying the

American practice of hiring blacks to work on their sleeping cars. When Daniel Peterson first arrived in Montreal, most men from the West Indies saw a job with the railroads as their best opportunity for full-time secure work.

The life of a porter was not easy, but any black man who got a job with the railroads was considered lucky. Within the black community there was status and prestige attached to working for the railroad. The men were treated with respect and admired for their clean uniforms.

In their own community, then, the Petersons were certainly not as badly off as some. In a neighborhood where everyone was poor, at least Daniel had a steady job. Sometimes the money ran out before his next pay day, but most of the time he brought in enough to feed his family and pay the rent.

As if the daily struggles of life weren't enough, the Petersons, like other West Indian blacks who had come to Montreal, had several difficult adjustments to make in their new country. For the first time in their lives, they were living in a place where black people were a minority of the population. They were also English speakers surrounded by a majority of French speakers within the province of Quebec.

Private organizations were formed to help the black population with the practical and spiritual concerns of everyday life. Some of these organizations provided food and clothing, while others found temporary shelter for those left homeless by unemployment. With the help of these organizations, the black residents of Montreal began to feel a sense of their own community. Two of these local institutions, the Union United Church and the Negro Community Centre, played important roles in the lives of the Peterson family.

The Petersons were hard-working, religious people. They loved the music they heard at church every week, and Daniel had always loved classical music. Olive also came from a musical family. Daniel and Olive showed little interest in the popular entertainment or music of the day. Daniel in particular frowned upon it, judging it to be immoral and corrupt.

As it happened, though, just when the Petersons were settling down to their new life in Montreal, the city was earning a reputation for being the jazz capital of the north. By the 1920s, Montreal had a thriving night life, where jazz was the music for dancing and partying. Montreal became an important stop for black musicians from across North America. The musicians saw the loose liquor laws and bustling club scene of the city as an opportunity for extra work. There were frequent jam sessions, where musicians would get together after their night's work and play until the early hours of the morning. It was in some of these clubs that Oscar Peterson would cut his musical teeth.

This is the background against which Olive and Daniel Peterson were raising a family in Montreal in the 1920s. For many of Montreal's black community, daily survival was a goal in itself. Earning enough to feed your family and keep a roof over their heads left little energy for dreaming or ambitious plans for the future. But Daniel Peterson was a fiercely proud and determined man. And as his family grew, so did his determination. He would do whatever he could to lift his children out of this life of limited opportunities, where they would likely become porters and housekeepers simply because of the color of their skin.

The children arrived in quick succession. First came Fred, then Daisy, Charles, Oscar and May. Daniel was grateful that in Canada his children would receive a good formal education, something that had not been possible for him.

Soon it was apparent that the Peterson children were gifted learners. All of them learned to read and write by the time they were three. His children remembered Daniel Peterson as a quiet, serious man. When he was not working, he could sit and play solitaire all day, a cigar in his mouth. Sometimes he would read a poem or the newspaper out loud, asking his kids to explain something he didn't understand. As Daisy Sweeney, Oscar's older sister, said, "He didn't have much [education] himself, but he had a hunger for it, always."

One time, when Daisy was six and her brother Fred was seven, the teacher gave them paper and told them to draw anything they wanted. "Fred and I decided to do long division and have a race doing it," Daisy remembered. "The teacher came around to see what we had done. The other children had drawn stick figures and trees or whatever you draw in grade one." When their teacher took them to the office, Daisy and Fred were scared, wondering what they had done wrong. They were relieved to discover that the teacher just wanted to show off their work to the other teachers.

As important as school was in the Petersons' lives, there was something that would become even more important. For Daniel Peterson, music became the tool through which his children would escape a life of serving others. He had little formal education, but music was something he could pass on to his kids. After all, hadn't he taught himself to play the organ with no help from anyone?

He set about to make his dream a reality. He had already begun to teach his wife to play the piano. Now, as his older children reached school age, he turned his attention to them.

2

No Ordinary Talent

When Oscar Emmanuel Peterson was born on August 15, 1925, the Petersons were living on Delisle Street in St. Henri, next door to the Union United Church. In those days, music formed an important part of everyday life for Montreal's black community. There was music at church, music at school and music in the home. "Music was the way we showed love to each other," one elderly Montrealer remembered. "A house was not a home until there was a piano in it."

Daisy Sweeney remembered listening to music coming from the church with her older brother, Fred, and singing along. Oscar was just a baby then, but Daisy said that the music "must have had some godly effect on him." By that time, she and Fred and Charles were already learning to play music themselves, and Oscar would soon join them. Daniel Peterson gave the older children piano lessons, and then he expected them to teach their younger siblings everything they had learned.

Daniel had decided that the children would each learn a second instrument as well. All five of them chose brass instruments — trumpet or trombone. When Oscar was five years old, he began to study piano and trumpet. His first teacher was ten-year-old Daisy, and in some ways she was the most important teacher he ever had. She could be kind and encouraging, but also firm when her little brother tried to get out of practicing. Throughout his life, Oscar has often praised his sister's teaching. He remembers how patient she was, and how she could relate to someone having difficulties and figure out ways to overcome them. From the start, Oscar saw that learning music was fun and challenging, and that made him want to learn more.

All the Peterson children showed considerable musical ability. With Oscar though, there was something special, as Daisy soon discovered. One day she was playing the piano when Oscar, who was sitting at the other end of the room, began to call out the names of the notes she had just played. Daisy was amazed and played something else. Again Oscar was able to name the notes without seeing them. This rare ability — to carry around the precise pitch of each note in your head — is called perfect pitch. People with perfect pitch know, without being told, that the note they've just heard is a G instead of a B.

Around this same time Daisy made another discovery. If Oscar made a mistake, he would want to start back at the beginning of the piece, even when she urged him to pick it up where he had left off. This puzzled her, until she realized that Oscar wasn't reading the music from the page at all. He was waiting until she played it, and then he would play it back by ear. In fact, the music on the stand might just as well have been a prop, for all Oscar was using it. Daisy realized that Oscar had a special gift, being able to hear music so well, but she knew from her own studies that the ability to read music notation was a valuable skill for any musician. After that Daisy didn't play anything for him until he had learned it from reading the notes himself.

But becoming a musician isn't just about having ability. Hard work and persistence are necessary to learning any musical instrument. Daniel Peterson knew this as well as anyone. He remembered how much practice it had taken him to learn to play the organ, and now he was determined to see that his children kept at their practice as well.

Daniel's job as porter meant that he was often away from home, yet he still managed to get his young family to practice even when he wasn't around to supervise. He would assign each of his children some music to learn while he was away, writing the task clearly beside each child's name in a book. When they had completed their assignment, they were expected to sign the book.

And the children knew their father meant business. There was no such thing as taking a week off because they were too busy with something else, or because they didn't feel like playing. They all knew the consequences of failing to do their father's bidding. For when Daniel came back from being on the road, he would call each of them into the piano room one by one and ask them to play their assignment. And by his side was a leather strap, just in case.

Some of the Peterson children fared better than others with this extreme teaching method. Daisy seems to have received the most beatings for failing to play up to her father's expectations. Maybe she could have recovered from the physical blows, but the emotional bruising she took left permanent marks. At first she had enjoyed playing for others, but as her father's criticism continued, she grew more and more unsure of herself.

One time, when she was preparing to play in a little recital, her father reminded her not to make any mistakes. He told her that if she made a mistake when she started to play, people would lose interest. Then he told her that if she made one at the end, that would undo all the good playing that had come before it. Daisy became so nervous that she made mistakes not only at the beginning and the end, but in the middle, too. From that time on, whenever she had to play in public, she was a bundle of nerves.

Daisy was unable to shrug off her father's harsh criticism. Oscar, though, had a very different personality. He would make his older siblings nervous by signing his name in the book before he had even looked at his assignment. They would say to him, "What did you sign the book for? You haven't practiced." But Oscar wasn't worried. He knew that if his father was gone for fourteen days, he could sit down on the twelfth and thirteenth days, listen to Daisy practice the assignment, and get it right away by ear. Sometimes, just to be absolutely sure, he would go to the piano and try it once through.

When Oscar and the other children played to their father's satisfaction, Daniel Peterson would say, "Fine, now here's what I want you to do next week." But Daniel was a hard man to please. Sometimes Oscar would be feeling really proud of something he had played, but instead of praising him, his father would remind him that there were other people who could do what he was doing, only much better. Oscar grew to realize that no matter how well he played, his father would be looking for faults. He was hurt by this, but he managed to show a self-confidence, even a brashness, that helped to cover the pain he was feeling.

Although the Petersons were not as poor as some others in their community, they were not able to afford much beyond the basic necessities. But there were the monthly payments Daniel had to make on the piano, and then there were the brass instruments the children were learning as well. Daisy remembered that one month there wasn't enough left for the piano payment, so the company threatened to seize the instrument. Either the children would go with less to eat, or the Petersons would lose their piano. Olive Peterson told her children to stay in bed so they wouldn't feel so weak from hunger, and they managed to get through the month. The piano stayed.

When Oscar was about seven, he joined his older siblings in a community band led by William Thomas, a bandmaster his mother knew from Halifax. The band met at the Peterson house for weekly rehearsals, followed by performances at church and at local community centers. Oscar played cornet and trumpet while Daisy played piano and trombone. There was an assortment of other instruments in the band, including tuba, clarinet and violin. The music they played was a classical band style, simple and full of repetition.

Daisy could see how bored Oscar was getting, playing the same part over and over. She saw him eyeing the clarinet player, who was given more interesting melodies to play. Next thing she knew, Oscar was making up his own melodies rather than playing the notes on the page. When the bandmaster heard what Oscar was doing, he yelled at him and told him to stick to his part. It would be years before Oscar was playing jazz, and yet already he was showing an interest in improvising, or making melodies up as he went along. Improvisation, of course, is one of the most important features of jazz music.

About this same time Oscar's older brother Fred began to experiment with a kind of music different from the classical pieces that he and his brothers and sisters had been learning. Oscar would stand beside his brother and listen intently, fascinated by the new sounds that were coming from the piano. Even the names of the tunes sounded strange to him — names like "Oh Dem Golden Slippers" and "Tiger Rag." He loved the lilting rhythms of the music — rhythms that made him want to dance when he heard them. Fred told him that this music was called jazz.

Daniel Peterson wasn't too pleased with the idea of his children playing jazz. At that time, many people considered jazz to be music best left to ignorant, uneducated people. Daniel Peterson's children would play classical music, not jazz.

Their mother however, was more supportive of the children's interest in jazz music. Olive was a soft-spoken, religious woman. She didn't have the force or presence of her husband, but in her own quiet way she had a great influence on the career paths of all her children, especially Oscar.

★ ★ ★

When he was still only seven years old, Oscar's music studies, and all the other normal activities of his life, came to a sudden and frightening halt. He became ill with tuberculosis, or TB, a serious disease that affects the lungs and is easily spread from person to person. In those days, people who got TB were put in the hospital, in a special area away from other people. Oscar spent thirteen months in Children's Memorial Hospital, recovering from his illness.

Thirteen months is a long time for anyone, but it is especially long when you are seven years old. When Oscar was finally able to go home, he was cured of TB, but his lungs had been weakened. His father decided that it would be best for him to give up playing the trumpet and concentrate on piano instead. His older brother Fred wasn't so lucky. Fred became sick with TB and died when he was just fifteen years old, in

1934. Oscar once said that Fred was the best pianist in the family. One can only imagine how good a musician he might have become.

After being sick for so long, Oscar was overjoyed to be able to play his piano again. It's hard to know for sure, though, how much he actually practiced when he was nine or ten or eleven years old. One reason is that Oscar, like many great story-tellers, has told many versions of his story, changing bits and pieces from one time to the next. He once said that he prac-ticed the piano from nine o'clock in the morning until noon. Then he would take an hour off for lunch, return to the piano and practice from one to six in the afternoon, and stop for his dinner. By seven-thirty at night he would be back at it again, only stopping when his mother dragged him away from the piano so the family could get some sleep.

This version of the story leaves out certain details. Oscar, like any other boy his age, had to go to school every day. Also, the other members of his family must have had some time at the piano themselves. In this version Oscar presented himself as a very studious, hard-working boy. It is quite a different pic-ture from the one Oscar gave when he said that he could sit around reading comic books and taking it easy for twelve days, and then learn his assignment the day before his father came home.

That Oscar loved to play the piano, there can be no doubt. When he became a professional musician, he got a reputation for being one of the hardest-working players around. We can imagine that he worked hard at his music, even when he was a child. At the same time, the evidence suggests that from a very young age, he was able to play so easily and so naturally that he didn't need to practice as much as his father expected him to.

Whether he practiced almost every waking moment of

every day or not, Oscar made extraordinary progress at the piano. When he was eleven, his father decided that it was time for him to take some lessons with someone outside the family. He called Lou Hooper, a pianist who had been part of the Harlem jazz scene in the 1920s, and who was now a well-known teacher in Montreal.

In his autobiography, Hooper described Oscar as a plump boy "looking very neat in an overly snug dark suit, buttoned up to the top and with knee-pants." He noted that Oscar, like all the other members of his family, was very polite and dignified.

Then Oscar sat down at the piano, and Lou Hooper was amazed at how well this eleven-year-old child could play, and how much he already knew. Oscar first played the pieces he was working on, and then he played scales and other technical exercises, all from memory. As Lou Hooper remembered, "He knew them all, as well as possessing nature's gift of perfect pitch, which I observed and tested fully."

Lou Hooper gave Oscar a few lessons, suggesting pieces for him to work on and coming to his home every couple of weeks to hear his progress. Oscar was already so skilled that he could make considerable progress on his own, without needing a teacher looking over his shoulder all the time.

Oscar enjoyed his lessons with Lou Hooper, but it was his next teacher, Paul Alexander de Marky, who would have an even greater influence on his development as a pianist. Daisy Peterson was already a student of de Marky, who was then considered one of the finest classical pianists in Canada. At some point she decided that Oscar should be studying with him as well, and without telling Oscar, she went ahead and booked a lesson for him.

In his autobiography, Oscar remembered his first meeting

with de Marky: "As the door opened I was faced with a small, almost frail-looking man, with intense eyes, sunken cheeks, and veined hands." De Marky led Oscar over to the piano and asked him to play something. Before Oscar could finish the piece, de Marky jumped up from his seat. "No, no! That's not the way you play Chopin," he announced, and he proceeded to show Oscar what he wanted.

This was the start of a long and important relationship in Oscar's life. De Marky had a huge impact on how Oscar played the piano as well as influencing his musical tastes and preferences.

De Marky was born in Hungary in 1897 and came to Canada in 1921. He came out of the tradition of the great Romantic pianists of the nineteenth century, which meant that he had a superb technique and a beautiful sound on the piano. Hungary's Franz Liszt was among the most brilliant and well known of the great European musicians who played in this style. Paul de Marky studied with Stefan Thoman, who was a student of Liszt.

By studying with de Marky, Oscar Peterson was continuing in the line of these master European pianists. He learned a way of playing the piano that would influence the way he played jazz. It was a very flashy style, full of lightning-quick runs up and down the keyboard. It demanded exceptional control in both the right and left hands, and Oscar came to have a reputation for having one of the most powerful left hands of any jazz pianist of his time.

From the time he was fourteen, Oscar immersed himself in learning this particular way of playing the piano. It was something that set him apart from most other jazz pianists.

Oscar's comments about Paul de Marky show the great impression de Marky made on him as a young player: "Paul de Marky came into my life at a very important time. I was fourteen. I went to this man. He totally awed me with his beautiful sound on the instrument, his beautiful touch, and his command of the instrument." Oscar was so inspired by his teacher that he would come to his lessons early. Then he would sit outside the room where de Marky was practicing, unaware that his young pupil was listening.

But Paul de Marky was extremely important to Oscar in another way. Unlike Oscar's father, de Marky showed no reservations about the jazz music that Oscar loved to play. At the end of each lesson, he would ask Oscar to play whatever jazz piece he was working on at that time. De Marky wasn't a jazz musician, but he gave Oscar valuable suggestions for making his playing more musical, more singing. When de Marky was an old man, he remembered teaching Oscar technique — "speedy fingers," as he said — "because that's what you need in modern jazz."

So at the tender age of fourteen, Oscar Peterson was developing a formidable technique at the piano, inspired by his classical studies with Paul de Marky. At the same time he was teaching himself the jazz songs he loved so much — songs that got his foot tapping and his heart pounding.

Then Daisy heard about a nationwide amateur radio contest sponsored by the Canadian Broadcasting Corporation (CBC). This was many years before the first televisions started to appear in North America. At that time families would entertain themselves by gathering around the radio and listening to their favorite programs.

The CBC in those days offered many different radio shows, including some with live music. This contest was a way of finding out about new musicians — young and talented and as yet undiscovered — who would then be hired to work on these shows.

Daisy thought Oscar should audition for the contest, but he hesitated. At that time he was still shy about playing for people, but Daisy finally convinced him to accompany her to the CBC studio. When they got there, she had to push Oscar onto the piano stool and urge him to play.

Oscar had nothing to worry about. As soon as the judge heard him, he gave him a spot on the radio program that same night. Oscar went on to win the semi-finals of the contest, and then the finals in Toronto.

Suddenly the fourteen-year-old boy from St. Henri was propelled into the public spotlight, where he has been ever since. Soon Oscar Peterson would be heard regularly on radio in Montreal and right across Canada. Soon he would be playing in bands around town and, within a few years, he would be leading his own trios in the best-known jazz clubs in Montreal. Oscar's star was shining bright, but there was much hard work ahead, and many obstacles to overcome. He was a brilliant pianist, but he was also black, and he was living in a world full of prejudice.

3

Learning the Jazz Tradition

Oscar Peterson's first-place finish in the CBC contest brought some dramatic changes to his life. He was given a weekly spot, called "Fifteen Minutes' Piano Rambling," on radio station CKAC in Montreal. And until 1945 he played on CBM, the English-language station of the CBC in Montreal, and on "The Happy Gang," a CBC national radio program. He was barely a teenager, but he was certainly living no ordinary teenage life.

All of this exposure on the airwaves made Oscar something of a celebrity, not only in his local neighborhoods of St. Henri and St. Antoine, but throughout the city of Montreal. Needless to say, his achievements got him a fair bit of attention at school as well.

Montreal High School was known not only for its excellent academic program, but also for its outstanding school band. When Oscar was a student there, he was the best known of several budding musicians. There were the Ferguson brothers — trumpeter Maynard and his saxophonist brother Percy — trombonist Jiro (Butch) Watanabe and bassist Hal Gaylor.

Maynard Ferguson would become a famous jazz trumpeter, and Butch Watanabe and Hal Gaylor also went on to successful jazz careers.

In his later high school years, Oscar played with the Montreal High School Victory Serenaders, a dance band led by Percy Ferguson. Daniel Peterson was not keen about his son playing in a jazz band, but once again Olive came to her son's defence. Maynard and Percy's father was a respected elementary school principal, and he was letting the band rehearse in a classroom at his school. Surely, Olive argued, there was nothing improper in that. Daniel gave in, and Oscar was allowed to join the band.

For all of Daniel's disapproval, it was clear that Oscar was focusing more and more of his attention on jazz. At that time there were very few black musicians playing classical music. But even if the classical concert stage had been more welcoming, Oscar would probably still have chosen to play jazz. He was bothered by the strictness and formality of classical music. He would find himself playing a piece and want to play it another way, to tinker with its melody and rhythm and harmony. Improvisation used to be part of classical music, but by the end of the eighteenth century it had become less common. In jazz, however, improvisation has almost always been very important.

There was something in Oscar's personality that was drawn to the creativity of jazz music. While he was still in his early teens, he began to listen to the early piano masters such as James P. Johnson, Thomas (Fats) Waller and Ferdinand (Jelly Roll) Morton, as well as to the generation of pianists that followed them, including Teddy Wilson and Art Tatum. By listening to them, he absorbed the jazz piano styles of the past while keeping up with the more modern sounds that were all around him.

Part of what Oscar was absorbing was not just the sounds of the individual players, but the language of jazz itself. He was learning about melody, harmony and rhythm as a jazz musician hears them. Most of the jazz performances he listened to followed a common form. The melody or theme of the tune — what jazz musicians call the "head" — was played first or sung by a vocalist. The improvisations or solos came next, and then the band returned to the head to end the tune.

Oscar discovered that in jazz there was greater room for interpretation than in traditional classical music. Decisions about rhythm, dynamics and phrasing — how a melody or line was shaped — were left to the individual player or band. Five jazz musicians playing the same tune could come up with five very different versions, and a musician might even interpret the same tune in different ways from one performance to the next.

After playing the head, the members of the band would take turns improvising, or soloing. (Some styles of jazz — Dixieland, for example — have featured collective improvisation, in which two or more players are improvising at the same time.) In a jazz solo or improvisation, a performer can explore different aspects of the tune, including the melody, the harmony (the chord changes of the tune), or the scales upon which a tune is based. Oscar learned the solos of his favorite players by copying what they were doing, and then he used things he liked in his own solos.

In his classical studies he had learned to play his eighth notes evenly. When he played jazz, he learned to swing his eighth notes — to hold the first of a pair of eighth notes longer than the second. The ability to play with that "swing feel" became very important for Oscar, and later it was something he looked for in any musician he hired. His great ears allowed him to hear the chord changes and voicings — the particular order of notes in a chord — that his favorite players were using, and these too became part of his own jazz vocabulary.

By the time Oscar was eleven, he had already learned his scales, chords and key signatures and understood the theory behind them. When he began to play jazz, he applied this knowledge to help him understand what his favorite pianists were playing, both in their solos and in their accompaniment.

For a young musician learning to play jazz in the 1940s, there were many piano styles to choose from. At that time a traditional jazz revival was underway and some players were going back to the styles that had been popular in the 1920s and 1930s. Some of these styles included boogie-woogie, stride and swing. Others were more interested in trying to play the modern style, called bebop.

Oscar saw no reason why he had to restrict himself to playing one style over another. Montreal wasn't too far from New York, at that time the city at the heart of jazz innovation. Oscar was able to keep on top of the newest trends in jazz, but he was far enough away that he didn't feel the pressure to have to play any particular way.

Oscar played boogie-woogie through his teen years and into his early twenties. Boogie-woogie developed first in the towns and countryside throughout the southern United States. The folk musicians who played this style were, for the most part, self-taught. Often they could not read music, and their playing was very simple — mostly blues or little melodies that they had worked out by ear. Since they had no formal training on the piano, they had trouble playing one thing with the left hand while they played something else with the right. They solved this problem by giving the bass, or left hand, a very simple figure, which they would play over and over.

The first boogie-woogie musicians weren't the most skilled players, but their music was powerful and full of feeling. Of course, Oscar Peterson played boogie-woogie with the same exceptional control of dynamics, tempo and execution that he brought to all his playing, so his boogie-woogie sounded very different from that of the untrained players. Oscar's first recordings were mainly in this boogie-woogie style. They are available now on compact disc, so it is possible to go back and hear how Oscar was playing when he was nineteen and twenty years old.

But at the same time, Oscar was also listening to the masters of stride piano — players such as Jelly Roll Morton, James P. Johnson and Fats Waller. The stride style kept a steady "oompah" feeling in the left hand, which played octaves on the first and third beats of each bar, with full chords on beats two and four. At the same time, the right hand would move deftly up and down the keyboard, playing rapid, tricky figures. The stride masters were excellent, well-trained musicians with solid backgrounds in classical piano. Stride is generally considered a much harder style to play, at least at an advanced level, than boogie-woogie. Stride piano didn't die out the way boogie-woogie did. Even today there are pianists, Oscar among them, who use elements of stride in their playing.

Oscar has always said that he was influenced by many piano players. No player, though, had a bigger effect on him than Art Tatum. Throughout his career, he has often repeated the story of how he first heard Tatum. It is a fascinating story, not only for showing the impact Tatum made on him, but also for what it reveals about Oscar's relationship with his father.

Oscar was getting a great deal of praise for someone of his age. There was a baby grand piano in the foyer of Montreal High School, and Oscar would sit there at lunchtime playing boogie-woogie and amazing his fellow students. With all this attention, it is not surprising that he was getting a bit of a swollen head.

Daniel Peterson noticed this and was not pleased. One day he came home and told Oscar there was a record he wanted him to hear. Oscar remembered that his father put it on: "I'll never forget — it was Art Tatum's *Tiger Rag*. And, truthfully, I gave up the piano for two solid months; and I had crying fits at night."

Oscar was crying from both fear and envy. Art Tatum was a truly masterful pianist, and Oscar could not imagine ever coming close to playing as well himself. At first he even had trouble believing that there was only one piano and not two. Oscar certainly wasn't the only musician to have this reaction to Tatum's playing.

Oscar wasn't scared of too many players — from a young age he knew how good he was — but Art Tatum was different. He left Oscar feeling awestruck, even afraid. Later on Oscar would meet him, and eventually they became close friends. Even so, it took Oscar a long time before he could feel relaxed around his idol.

Oscar lost some of his arrogance after his father exposed him to the music of Art Tatum. Happily, though, he recovered from this humbling experience and took up the challenge. If anything, it made him determined to work even harder, so that one day he might be able to play the things he was hearing in Tatum's music.

Before Oscar was old enough to be hanging out in Montreal's jazz clubs, he did most of his learning by listening to records and to the radio. Daniel Peterson had saved up for months to buy his family a radio, which had a place of prominence in the living room. Late at night, after the rest of them had gone to bed, Oscar would tiptoe downstairs and turn it on. Keeping the volume low so he wouldn't disturb anyone, he would press his ear against the speaker and listen to live broadcasts of the great swing bands. In this way he heard Count Basie and Duke Ellington, Jimmie Lunceford and Chick Webb.

Any student of jazz knows that the only way to learn jazz is to listen to the music. The way that jazz musicians use rhythm, tone and phrasing is often difficult, if not impossible, to represent accurately through musical notation. Oscar's late-night listening sessions were as important to his development as a jazz musician as his formal lessons with Paul de Marky were to his classical training.

Oscar would also buy records of his favorite artists. The bassist Hal Gaylor, a schoolmate at Montreal High School, remembered going to Oscar's house and listening to records with him. On one of these records was a young bass player named Ray Brown. Oscar used to tell his friend, "Some day I'm going to have a trio, and he's going to be my bass player." As time would tell, there was more to Oscar's words than youthful boasting.

★ ★ ★

Oscar's family had always been closely connected with the local church and community organizations of Montreal's black population. As Oscar got older, he became more personally involved with them through his music.

One of these institutions was the Negro Community Centre, originally called the Negro Community Association. It was established in 1927 by Reverend Charles Este, one of the great leaders of Montreal's black community. Este had moved to Montreal from the West Indies and became pastor of the Union United Church, the same church the Petersons lived beside on Delisle Street when Oscar was born.

Reverend Este wanted to improve the everyday lives of black people in his community. He wanted them to feel better about themselves, to have more confidence that they could do something meaningful with their lives. He knew they would have to come together as a community in order to face their daily struggle against prejudice and discrimination. To that end, he invited famous black men and women from all over the world to speak at the Negro Community Centre.

One of the speakers was Marcus Garvey, a Jamaican who believed that blacks and whites should live separate from each other. He even thought that black people would be better off going back to Africa, where they were originally from, instead of trying to fit in with a white society that didn't seem to want them. Garvey moved to the United States in 1916 to promote his beliefs. For the next twenty years he was one of the most famous and controversial black men in the world.

Many blacks liked what Marcus Garvey was saying. He made them feel proud of their African heritage, proud of being black. For some, this was a feeling they had never experienced before. Many others, though, including most Canadian blacks, did not agree with Garvey's views on separation.

As a teenager, Oscar Peterson played piano every Sunday afternoon during meetings at the Negro Community Centre. He remembered Marcus Garvey telling them to become purposeful, to work hard to learn other skills so they would not have to be railway workers forever. In this respect, Garvey was saying what Oscar's father had been telling his children all along. These words stayed with Oscar, even if he did not believe in Garvey's message that blacks and whites should live apart.

As time went on, Oscar began to pay more attention to his music than to his schoolwork. It's not that he was doing poorly at school; in fact, he generally got excellent grades. But music was his passion. It was what he lived and breathed for. Nothing that he was learning at school came close to matching the love he had for playing his piano.

Before long, Oscar was hanging out at St. Antoine's jazz clubs, in the black part of the district. In the 1940s, there were several places offering jazz within this one small area where Mountain Street and St. Antoine met. This area came to be known as The Corner. Some of the older musicians on The Corner began to look out for Oscar. Now and then they would let him play a tune or two. Jazz musicians call this "sitting in."

Oscar's musical skills were developing quickly, but his school studies seemed less and less important to the rest of his life. After thinking it over, he made a big decision. He would ask his father to let him quit school. He knew this was no small matter. His parents had always stressed the importance of education, and now he was thinking about quitting even before he had finished high school.

Oscar summoned up his courage and went to talk to his father. He told him that he was no longer interested in his high school studies, that he wanted to devote all his time to studying music. He remembered that his father looked at him for a minute, and then he said, "There are a lot of jazz piano players out there. You just going to be another one of them?" Oscar didn't reply. He wasn't sure what to say. At last his father spoke again. "I can't let you leave high school to be a jazz piano player. If you want to be the best, I'll let you go. But you have to be the best, there is no second best."

Once again Daniel Peterson was challenging his son, as he had earlier when he brought home the Art Tatum record. By now he had resigned himself to the fact that Oscar had his heart set on jazz, not classical music. Still, he was making it clear that his standards had not changed, that he would not be satisfied with mediocrity, with doing something only as well as most people around you. Daniel demanded that his children stand out, that they be — in his mind, anyway — better than the people around them. If Oscar couldn't be the best jazz pianist, then he shouldn't bother being one at all.

Many people would argue that in music or art or dance, there is no such thing as the best. They would say that there is room for many artists to share the spotlight. After all, one person might offer something that is not necessarily better than what another person can offer, just different.

But if Daniel Peterson had felt this way, Oscar might not have approached his music with such a fierce determination to be the best jazz piano player around. For one thing is sure. Oscar has always seen music as a competition where there really is such a thing as being the best. Oscar has called it a friendly competition, even a loving one, and he has been quick to praise those musicians whose work he respects. He has never stood by, though, and let another player challenge his playing without wanting to answer the call.

Soon after his talk with his father, Oscar left Montreal High School and embarked on the next stage of his young life. He set out to become a professional jazz musician.

Art Tatum (1909–1956)

Arthur Tatum, Jr., was born in Toledo, Ohio, in 1909. He was almost blind from birth, even though he had several operations to remove cataracts from his eyes. Both his parents played music, and they saw music as a way for Art to earn a living. He took classical lessons at a young age, and eventually he studied at several music schools in Ohio.

Art Tatum was a musical genius. He approached the piano as if it were an orchestra, playing melodies, harmonies and rhythms with such independence of his hands that when Oscar Peterson first heard Tatum on record, he was sure there was more than one pianist at work. Tatum had an astonishing ability to hear, and a deep understanding of harmony. Quickly he became a legend among musicians.

Tatum did not invent a specific piano style. Instead, he took things he liked from existing styles and put them together in his own way. He gave Fats Waller credit for being one of his main influences, but Waller himself introduced Tatum one night with these words: "Ladies and gentlemen," Waller said, "I play piano, but God is in the house tonight."

Tatum kept some of the stride sound in his playing, but he also used elements from another style made popular by the pianist Earl Hines. Hines, unlike the stride players, played melody lines in his right hand in the style of a horn. Later on this came to be called the "trumpet style" of playing piano.

Tatum also played these long melodic lines in the right hand and moving chords in the left. But unlike any other player before him, he would interrupt the pattern he was playing with sudden, quick dashes up and down the keyboard. These dashes were often out of tempo, breaking the flow of the music. Not everyone admired this about Tatum's playing; some said he was showing off at the expense of keeping a steady beat. For most musicians, though, Art Tatum was a master pianist without equal.

4

The Corner

By the time Oscar was in his mid-teens, he had worked up a strict practice routine. In the morning he played scales, exercises and classical pieces. In the afternoon he practiced voicings, trying out different ways to connect one chord to the next within a song.

At a certain point he realized that there were things he wanted to play that consistently gave him trouble. The melodies and ideas were there in his head, but he would stumble when he tried to execute them on the piano. So he sat down and went through these problem areas slowly and methodically, trying to figure out ways to overcome them.

He came up with some exercises to increase the control and independence of his hands. He would keep a steady tempo in his right hand and let his left hand play with a looser time feel, and then he would repeat the exercise, this time making his left hand keep the tempo while his right hand played against the time.

In improvisation, the ability to think ahead is crucial. Oscar practiced playing one phrase while working out in his head what he wanted to play next. Soon his phrases became more connected and his improvisations more fluent. He was like someone learning a foreign language. As his control of vocabulary and grammar increased, he had an easier time telling his story, which he expressed not through words, but through melody, harmony and rhythm.

He practiced for hours at a stretch, day after day, and soon he found himself gaining control of these problem areas. By the time he was sixteen or seventeen, he was able to play almost anything that came into his head.

When he was not at home practicing, Oscar was hanging out on The Corner. He was still under age, so by law he should not have been allowed in the clubs at all. But he went back night after night, drawn to the smoke-filled, noisy clubs by the wonderful music he heard coming from inside.

One musician in particular took Oscar under his wing. Harold (Steep) Wade was a big gruff man with a stern expression. He was the star jazz pianist in the Montreal area from the late thirties through the forties, the favorite accompanist of many players in town. Even though he wasn't the flashiest of players, he could play well in several different styles and knew a large number of tunes.

For a time Wade was the house pianist at Rockhead's Paradise, one of the jazz clubs on The Corner. Oscar thought of Wade as his musical godfather. "First of all," Oscar said, "Rockhead's wasn't exactly in the safest part of town. I used to go there every night just to hear the guys play. They used to sneak me in because I was under age at the time. Steep used to call me 'kid.'"

Steep Wade might have been a big tough man, but he had

a warm spot for the teenage boy who displayed such outstanding ability on the piano. He would let Oscar sit in for him when he needed a break or wanted to go to hear another player down the street. Steep would say to Oscar, "Okay, kid, go on and play the show for me. I'll be back."

Then Oscar would find himself on the bandstand, thrown into the fire of live jazz performance. He would be expected to play any tune that the other musicians might call, in any key or at any tempo, even if he was playing it for the first time.

Up to this point, Oscar's playing experience had been quite limited. He had played in his high school band, the Victory Serenaders, as well as at church and at the Negro Community Centre. Now Steep Wade was giving him a chance to play in a real jazz setting — an experience that no amount of practice can replace. It was in that environment — in a smoky club in St. Antoine — that Oscar really served his jazz apprenticeship. For a jazz musician, this on-the-job training is a necessary step on the road to becoming a professional.

But Oscar also learned a great deal just by listening to the older pianist. Steep Wade had a wonderful sense of time — that swinging feel, or bounce, that a jazz musician brings to the music. The best players all have this, although they may express it in different ways. Playing with good time is one of the most important skills a jazz player can have. By listening so carefully to Wade, Oscar absorbed that sense of time, that driving force, which is such a feature of his playing.

Café St. Michel was another popular club on The Corner where Oscar spent many hours as a teenager, listening and playing. Steep Wade played there with saxophonist Hugh Sealey's orchestra, and later with trumpeter Louis Metcalf. Wade would look out for Oscar, and as Oscar came toward the bandstand, he would give him a nod. Then he'd get up from the piano, walk away and say, "You got it," and Oscar would get more of that on-the-job training.

Despite his achievements as a player, Wade had the problem that affected so many jazz musicians of his era — he was addicted to drugs and alcohol. By early 1953 he was in very bad health from his addictions, and he died later that same year of heart failure. He was only thirty-five years old.

Steep Wade was one of many musicians Oscar would know in his long career whose life was cut short by the curse of drugs. It has never made sense to Oscar to give up so much for something that could only destroy you in the end. Oscar has never drunk much himself, nor has he been interested in taking drugs. His worst vices have been cigarettes and overeating. Most jazz musicians of his era smoked cigarettes, and Oscar has always loved and appreciated good food and fine dining. He is a big man with a big appetite.

★ ★ ★

Oscar was gaining valuable playing experience in the clubs of St. Antoine. Even so, it was clear that his talents were too enormous to be contained within one small area of Montreal. Word of the teenage piano sensation began to spread. When he was seventeen, he was invited to audition for the Johnny Holmes Orchestra, at that time the best-known big band in Montreal.

Holmes was a trumpet player and arranger who hired many talented young players for his band through the 1940s. This was an excellent opportunity for Oscar to play with some of Montreal's finest musicians. At the audition, Oscar was so keen on impressing Holmes that he played every flashy line he could think of in the very first tune. "He already had amazing technique," Holmes said later about that first rehearsal, "but he shot everything in the first chorus."

Holmes realized that Oscar was nervous, and he pulled him aside during the break. He explained to him that the role of a big-band pianist was to support the brass and reed sections, rather than to dominate the band. He told Oscar to play like Joe Bushkin, the piano player in Tommy Dorsey's band, one of the leading white big bands in the States. Oscar had listened to the Dorsey band, so he knew exactly what Holmes was looking for. "He got it right the first time," Holmes said. "He played just like Bushkin."

In 1942 Oscar left the Victory Serenaders to join Johnny Holmes. Every Saturday night the Holmes Orchestra played at Victoria Hall, in a wealthy part of Montreal called Westmount. The band also played private parties for well-to-do Montrealers. Holmes worked hard to make his band stand out from the other swing bands in Montreal. Instead of using stock arrangements — published arrangements of hit songs that most of the local bands used — he did his own arrangements.

When Oscar first joined the orchestra, he was, according to Johnny Holmes, "a diamond in the rough." Holmes had no questions about Oscar's physical ability, but he felt that Oscar was suffering from the problem that many young virtuosos have. He had developed so quickly, and he could play with such dazzling speed and flash, that he hadn't bothered to learn to play any other way.

Holmes invited Oscar over to his apartment to play through some of the band's music, and quickly the two men became friends. They began to meet regularly, with Holmes acting as musical adviser and coach. The hours that Oscar spent alone with Johnny Holmes were invaluable to his growth as a jazz musician.

Holmes would put on a record to make a point about jazz

phrasing, or to have Oscar listen to how the band's pianist was playing behind the soloist. He also worked with Oscar on the slow numbers, the beautiful ballads that the Holmes band featured.

As Steep Wade had been before him, Johnny Holmes became Oscar's mentor, helping him to play with more sensitivity and refinement. "[Johnny Holmes] is responsible for building up my technique," Oscar said a few years after he joined the band. "He really broke me all apart when I started with him. I was overdoing boogie-woogie and was completely at a loss for slow music. He showed me the style I'm using today."

Oscar stayed with Johnny Holmes until 1947. At various points, Holmes acted as his employer, manager and teacher. Those years were very important in his musical development, and they might have been smooth and trouble-free, except for one thing. Oscar Peterson was the only black player in the Johnny Holmes Orchestra.

The black population of Montreal was very small, and most of Oscar's fans at that time were white. They admired him for the brilliant playing he brought to the orchestra, and they treated him with the same respect they gave any of the white musicians in the band. There were some whites, however, who were not so tolerant. These people simply thought that a black person had no business playing in a white band. Time and again, Oscar would be reminded that no matter how well he played, to some he was first and foremost a black man in a society run by whites.

Discrimination was not new to Oscar. He had already experienced it at school, and he grew up in a black community that suffered as a result of it. And now in his work he was facing it again.

By 1945, Oscar had been with Johnny Holmes for three years. The orchestra was scheduled to play several engagements at the Ritz-Carlton Hotel, one of Montreal's most elegant and pricey establishments. Two days before the first date, the hotel manager called Johnny Holmes and said that he didn't want a "nigger" in his hotel. When Oscar found out, he waited to see how his boss would react. If Holmes suggested replacing him for the night, Oscar would consider quitting the band. He had made quite a name for himself by that time, and he wasn't about to suffer the indignity of such a situation.

But Johnny Holmes insisted that Oscar be allowed to play, or he would cancel the engagements. Then he threatened to put notices in Montreal's English-language newspapers, saying that the band could never play the Ritz because the hotel didn't allow blacks. The manager backed down, and the Johnny Holmes Orchestra played the dates, with Oscar at the piano.

The incident left Oscar with an uneasy feeling. He was glad to have the chance to play where black people had never been welcome before. He hoped that his experience would make it easier for the next person who had to face the same kind of situation. He worried, though, that people were making exceptions for him because he played so well. Maybe the doors would again be slammed shut once he had left.

★ ★ ★

Music was the most important thing in Oscar Peterson's life, but it wasn't the only thing. For some time he had been noticing a girl at church and in the social clubs the church ran for its members. Her name was Lillie Fraser, and she lived with her family in Verdun, not far from St. Antoine, where the Peterson family was now living. Her father, William Fraser, was also a porter for the Canadian Pacific Railway.

Oscar was drawn to the quiet girl with the long black hair. "I just fell in love with her," he said, "that soft, warm, straight-ahead person." In March of 1943, Hilton Braithwaite, a high school friend of Oscar's, took him to Lil's house so that Oscar could be formally introduced to her parents. Soon Oscar and Lil were seeing more and more of each other — going steady, as they called it in those days. Lil found Oscar charming. Even though he was only a teenager, in her eyes he looked and thought like a man. "Certainly," she remembered later, "his wonderful music was enough to turn any girl's head."

A few months later, Lil was at home when Oscar rang the bell. Lil opened the door and found him standing there with the presents he usually brought for her on these visits. She could tell, though, that he had something else on his mind. Finally he got to the point. He told her he was sure that some good breaks would be coming his way with his music, and that he really wanted to share them with her. Then he said he loved her, and that he would be able to support her. "So, let's you and me get married," he said.

Oscar pulled out a ring and put it on her finger, and Lil was thrilled. After he had left, she went around the neighborhood showing the ring to all her friends. On that day — August 15, 1943 — Oscar Peterson turned eighteen years old.

Just over a year later, in September 1944, Oscar and Lil were married at the Union United Church. The groom was nineteen and the bride was seventeen. Later Lil admitted that both of their mothers thought they were too young to get married.

Oscar might have been a married man, but a quiet home life was not in his plans. By 1944 his piano playing was starting to attract attention outside his home province of Quebec.

Jazz fans across the country were tuning in to the CBC national radio broadcasts featuring Oscar and his boogie-woogie, and they loved what they heard. World War Two was dragging on, and Oscar's bright and happy music was a welcome relief for people weary of hearing bad news, day after day, from Europe and other parts of the world.

Sometimes the CBC announcers would interview Oscar before or after he played a number. The entire show, including the interview, would be recorded. One of these interviews came from a 1944 appearance Oscar made on "The Merchant Navy Show." The announcer, Rusty Davis, introduced Oscar by saying, "Friends, tonight we'd like you to meet a colored boy whose amazing fingers have been cutting a rhythmic path to success over the airwaves for the past three years now." When Oscar had finished playing, Davis continued, "Oscar, that was terrific! Tell me, boy, how many hands you got?"

At that time, it seems to have been okay for the CBC announcer to call his guest a "colored boy." In those days, "boy" was a racist way of referring to a black person of any age. To call someone "boy" instead of "man" was a way of showing him less respect.

And a trained CBC announcer would never say "how many hands you got?" He would say, "How many hands do you have?" Rusty Davis was trying to talk "black" because he was sure that Oscar must talk "black." There is nothing wrong with talking black, or any way in particular, but it is racist to believe that a person must talk a certain way because of how he looks.

In fact, because Oscar Peterson went to school with people from all different ethnic backgrounds, he doesn't talk especially "black." He talks like someone who went through the English-language school system in Montreal. Oscar once said that he found those early CBC Radio interviews insulting. He got through them by keeping his mind on his goal. In those days he knew of no other black artist who was appearing on local radio. He knew he had the ability to go right to the top with his music, and that is where he was aiming. He wanted to get to where he "had some clout."

Racial prejudice was a fact of life for black people in Canada at that time, yet musicians from the United States liked coming north to escape the discrimination they were facing at home. At least when they came to Montreal, black and white musicians were able to play together on the same stage. This was still not possible in many parts of the States.

Oscar was especially happy to hang out at the clubs when the American players came to town. At the Café St. Michel in January 1944, he joined an early-morning jam session with musicians from the Count Basie Orchestra. At that time, the Basie Orchestra was one of the most famous big bands in the world. Later on, Basie said that he had never heard the ivory-box (the piano) played that way by a youngster. After Basie's visit, the jazz magazine *Down Beat* ran an article called, "Count Basie raves about young Canadian pianist."

Oscar began receiving more and more praise. On their visits to Montreal in the 1940s, Count Basie, Jimmie Lunceford, Frankie Newton, Mezz Mezzrow and Coleman Hawkins — all of them well-known American jazz musicians — heard Oscar play and were so impressed that they urged him to move to the States. Jimmie Lunceford was a successful big-band leader who even offered him a job in his band, but Oscar was still in high school and turned him down.

Even then, Oscar showed a remarkable ability to know just when to make his next move. He could have left for the United States right then, as did other Canadian jazz musicians of his era, in search of better career opportunities. But he had a couple of reasons for staying in Canada. His career was taking off, and he had as many playing opportunities as he could manage. He also loved Canada. He was proud to be Canadian, proud to be from Quebec.

So he decided to stay put. He would get all the playing experience he could in Canada, and when the time was right, he would go to the States. He trusted himself to know when that would be.

By 1944 Oscar was leading his own bands. One of them, the Tophatters, played at Wood Hall in Verdun. Another trio, with bassist Brian McCarthy and drummer Frank Gariépy, played on local radio. At the same time, Oscar continued to refine his style, to listen to other jazz pianists and learn from them. Two players in particular were to have a great influence on his later, more mature style.

One of them was Teddy Wilson, who played piano in the Benny Goodman Quartet and accompanied some of the greatest players of his time. Wilson was a swing player, but he played more complicated harmonies than many of his contemporaries. Because of that, he had a big influence on the new music, bebop. Oscar loved the way Teddy Wilson could play with both "fire and finesse."

Then, later on, he heard Nat (King) Cole, the great jazz singer and pianist. For Oscar, it was a defining moment. He heard Nat Cole and thought, "That's it. That's the kind of group I want." Nat Cole's singing and playing had that driving swing that Oscar had heard earlier in his mentor, Steep Wade. But Cole could also play with delicacy, in the manner of Teddy Wilson. Nat Cole's trio was one of the most popular jazz bands of its time.

Oscar Peterson was only twenty years old in 1945, but he

had already accomplished more than many musicians do in a lifetime. He could play with almost flawless virtuosity in two extremely different musical forms, classical and jazz. He had several years of professional playing experience under his belt, and he had met, played and studied with some of the best musicians of his time.

He knew he was ready to make his first recording. In his usual determined way, he set about to make that happen.

Nat King Cole (1917–1965)

From the early 1940s until his death in 1965, Nat King Cole was one of the most popular singers in America. He was born Nathaniel Adams Coles in Montgomery, Alabama, and his family moved to Chicago when he was four. Nat and his three brothers were gifted musicians, and all of them went on to have careers in music. Their father was a pastor, and as a youngster Nat played organ and sang in his father's church.

Nat first learned to play the piano by ear, but when he was a teenager he studied classical piano. His preference was for jazz, though, and he quickly fell under the influence of the outstanding jazz pianist Earl Hines. When Nat formed his own groups — the Rogues of Rhythm and the Twelve Royal Dukes — he used many of Hines's arrangements.

In 1936 Nat moved to Los Angeles, where he formed a trio called King Cole and his Swingsters — later called the King Cole Trio — with Oscar Moore on guitar and Wesley Prince on bass. Nat's choice of guitar instead of drums was unusual and influenced the instrumentation of several later trios, including, of course, Oscar Peterson's.

In 1943 Nat Cole went from being a jazz singer to a pop star with his hit song "Straighten Up and Fly Right." Before this recording, he had often sung with his trio, but this time he sang solo. His voice was smooth and delicate and appealed to both black and white audiences. After this hit he worked more often as a soloist backed by studio orchestra, and his later trios and quartets were there mainly in supporting roles, accompanying him while he sang.

Nat King Cole was a pioneer among black jazz artists. From 1948 to 1949 he had his own weekly radio show — one of the first black jazz musicians to be given this opportunity — and in the mid-1950s he hosted his own television show on NBC. Because he achieved such fame as a singer and entertainer, his talent as a jazz pianist often went unrecognized outside the jazz world.

Among jazz musicians, however, he was respected for his assured, fluent piano style. He combined the complicated right-hand technique he learned from Earl Hines with a swinging, rhythmic left-hand technique that owed much to the style of Count Basie. In the early 1940s, Nat Cole made several recordings that demonstrate what a good jazz pianist he was, including four with saxophonist Lester Young and bassist Red Callender.

Cole was an important influence on many jazz pianists who followed him, including Erroll Garner, Red Garland, Bill Evans and Oscar Peterson.

5

Escaping the Railroad

In the 1940s, the record industry was well established in the United States, but in Canada it lagged far behind. Even though Oscar Peterson was already well known in Canada, he wasn't sure how to go about getting a record contract. He went to his mother for advice.

"Call up a record company," she suggested, "and tell them you want to make a record."

Olive Peterson's advice was simple enough, but it worked. Oscar called Hugh Joseph, the head of RCA Victor in Canada. As it happened, Joseph had been hearing a great deal about the brilliant young pianist in the Johnny Holmes band. He later said that he likely would have gone after Oscar if Oscar had not approached him first. Soon the two of them had a contract that would see Oscar make more than a dozen records for the company during the next four years.

In those days, records were two-sided discs containing one short song or piece of music on each side. Each one of these individual recordings was known in the business as a "side." The records themselves were called 78s. The number referred to the rpm, or revolutions per minute, at which the record would turn.

The first side Oscar recorded was a popular tune of the day written by George Gershwin, called "I Got Rhythm." He went on to record eight sides in 1945, six of which were entirely or mainly in the boogie-woogie style. In the two or three years that followed, he continued to record boogie-woogie, although he began to mix in some stride and swing. In some of these recordings, it is possible to hear the influence of Nat Cole, Art Tatum and Teddy Wilson on his playing.

Oscar takes most of the tunes at very fast tempos. There are some brilliant moments on these first sides, especially when we remember that he was only nineteen or twenty when many of them were made. As a whole, though, they show a roughness and lack of maturity compared to the music he was putting out only a few years later.

But why was Oscar Peterson recording so much boogie-woogie, when his real goal was to become a recognized jazz pianist? After all, boogie-woogie wasn't even taken seriously by most jazz players or their fans. It was considered a more popular kind of music, far less interesting than the stride or swing or bebop that the true jazz musicians played. Later on, Oscar himself admitted that these early recordings didn't even represent what he was actually playing at the time.

At this point in his career, Oscar was torn. He could keep playing boogie-woogie, with its larger audiences and financial rewards, or he could concentrate on jazz. Oscar was a great boogie-woogie player, and he kept his fans screaming for more. His heroes, though, were Art Tatum, Nat Cole and Teddy Wilson — some of the best jazz pianists of their time. In his heart, he had his sights set on them.

By the time Oscar gave an interview to the Vancouver *Sun*

newspaper in 1946, he seemed to know that his days of playing boogie were coming to an end. "My first two boogie records seem to have typed me," he said. "But even if it's good commercially, I can't play boogie all my life. We had a big argument about it at Victor. They said 'Peterson, do you want to be a good commercial musician or do you want to be a collector's item?' I said collector's item!"

Between April 1945 and July 1946, Oscar recorded sixteen tunes for RCA Victor. The bassist for all of them was Bert Brown, but Oscar used several different drummers on these recordings. Through his records, radio broadcasts and club performances, he was quickly establishing himself as the up-and-coming jazz musician on the Canadian scene. On the whole, his future looked bright.

Just before Christmas, in 1945, Oscar went shopping in downtown Montreal. He decided to take a cab home, and when he saw one stop to drop off a passenger, he hurried over to it and started to step inside. At that moment a woman came up and demanded the same taxi. The man who had just stepped out of the cab called Oscar a "dirty nigger" and punched him in the face.

Oscar fell down and the woman took Oscar's place in the cab, which then drove away. A policeman was standing nearby and witnessed the entire incident, but he did nothing. Frustrated and angry, Oscar got up and knocked down the man who had struck him. The two exchanged blows, until the policeman finally stepped in and tried to arrest Oscar. Oscar stood his ground. "You turned your back when he hit me," he said to the policeman. "If you want to take me to the station, you'll have to use that gun."

At six feet two inches tall and just under two hundred and fifty pounds, Oscar Peterson was a formidable sight. The policeman just stood and watched in silence as Oscar picked up his parcels and walked away.

★ ★ ★

Oscar enjoyed a good deal of commercial success in 1946. For the first time, he traveled outside of Quebec to perform. In March he appeared at the Auditorium in Winnipeg, playing before four thousand enthusiastic fans. Then he continued on to Toronto, where he did a concert at Massey Hall. Many in the audience had heard him on his regular CBC broadcasts. Now they had their first chance to see him in person.

During that summer he was featured on a fifteen-minute weekly spot on a national CBC radio show. His popularity grew, and in September he began a five-city tour of western Canada. Instead of taking his own band with him, he played with the local dance band at each stop along the route.

When Oscar returned to Montreal, he went back to his regular jobs with Johnny Holmes and the other small groups he was leading. By now he was the star attraction and featured soloist in the Holmes band, which was being billed as the Johnny Holmes Orchestra with Oscar Peterson. Now that Oscar was the featured performer, he was earning enough money to make his living just from playing with the orchestra.

Then Holmes came up with another idea to highlight Oscar. For the last fifteen minutes of every dance, he let Oscar play with the band's bass player and drummer, while the rest of the orchestra sat out. The other musicians had a little routine going with Oscar during his feature. As Johnny Holmes explained, "We just let Oscar play… But he'd be playing, say, 'Body and Soul,' and someone in the band would call out another tune, say 'I Surrender Dear.' And he'd have to incorporate that right away into 'Body and Soul.' He never got hung up once. The band idolized him. The greatest audience he had was the band."

But Johnny Holmes also knew that in musical terms, Oscar was outgrowing the band. He talked to Oscar, urging him to explore other playing opportunities. For a long time Oscar was reluctant to leave. He felt comfortable and secure with the Johnny Holmes Orchestra, and he had a deep sense of loyalty to the man who had done so much for him.

By the fall of 1947, though, he decided to leave the orchestra and start his own trio. He began rehearsing at his house with Austin Roberts on bass and Clarence Jones on drums. Soon they had an offer to play at the Alberta Lounge, on the ground floor of the Alberta Hotel in downtown Montreal. Oscar and his trio would stay there for the next two years, with guitarist Bernard Johnson eventually replacing Jones.

Musicians often refer to the work they get as their gigs. For a jazz musician in Montreal at this time, the Alberta Lounge was considered one of the best gigs in town. For fifteen minutes every Wednesday night, radio station CJAD did live broadcasts of the trio from the Alberta Lounge. The more exposure Oscar got, the more other musicians were becoming aware of his enormous talent. During his time at the Alberta Lounge, it wasn't unusual for some of the jazz greats of that period to drop by the lounge to hear Oscar play and sit in with him.

Dizzy Gillespie, the famous bebop trumpet player, came to Montreal to play during that period. One night after work Oscar went to hear Dizzy play, and Dizzy invited him up on stage. Gerry Macdonald, a saxophonist in the Johnny Holmes band, remembered that Oscar sat down at the piano and began an introduction to "What Is This Thing Called Love?" — a popular jazz standard of the day. Dizzy had never heard Oscar play before. According to Macdonald, his eyes opened wide with disbelief as he listened. Oscar took a long solo, and the audience went crazy, screaming with delight.

After the gig, Oscar and Dizzy went to an after-hours club and stayed up all night playing. Oscar remembered that Dizzy's astonishment continued. He kept asking Oscar, "Do you really hear them chords?"

Oscar continued to visit his old haunts. After he finished his last set at the Alberta Lounge, he would walk over to The Corner and sit in at Rockhead's Paradise or Café St. Michel. Often he would play with the Sealey Brothers or Louis Metcalf's International Band, two of Montreal's finest jazz bands at that time. His old mentor, Steep Wade, was still playing there, and Oscar would sit and talk music with him.

But for Oscar, playing at the Alberta Lounge had a meaning beyond the music itself. Right across the street was Windsor Station, which was owned by the Canadian Pacific Railway, his father's employer. As Oscar sat at the piano, he had only to look out the window to be reminded of the life that might have awaited him — the life of a railway porter — if he had not become a musician.

Daniel Peterson had at times been a stern and harsh father, but his resolve remained firm. He would see that his children worked hard at school and at their music. Through hard work, he believed, they would escape a life of poverty, a life of serving others. Oscar was barely out of his teens, but it was becoming clear that music would be his future and his livelihood. He would not have to work on the railroad like his father.

Throughout his life, Oscar has shown complicated feelings about his father. He was hurt that his father would sooner criticize him than praise him. He was confused by his father's demands for perfection, even when it was clear that perfection was not possible. At the same time, though, Oscar always seemed to know that Daniel Peterson did what he did because he loved his children and wanted them to have a better life.

Sadly, not all of them fared as well as Oscar. Years earlier, the family had lost Fred, the oldest child, to tuberculosis. Oscar had another older brother, Chuck, who also wanted to be a professional pianist. Chuck played the trumpet as well as the piano, and he was in the army band through most of World War Two. When he was discharged from the army after the war, he wanted to go back to playing the piano, but music jobs were hard to find.

As a temporary job, Chuck got work in an aluminum plant. Something got stuck in the drop press where he was working, and he reached in with his arm to try to loosen the object. The press slammed down, crushing his arm below the elbow. Chuck went on to have a career in music as a trumpet player, because it is possible to play the trumpet with just one hand. His career as a pianist, though, was over.

Daisy Peterson, who became Daisy Peterson Sweeney after she married, decided to pursue a career as a music teacher rather than performer. For many years she worked as a domestic, putting aside a large portion of her wages toward her music lessons. She studied with Paul de Marky at McGill Conservatory, and in 1947, she earned an associate degree in music from McGill University.

Daisy gained a reputation as one of Montreal's leading piano teachers. Several of her students went on to distinguished careers in jazz, including Oliver Jones, Milton Sealey and Joe Sealy. In 1987, she was awarded an honorary doctorate by Laurentian University in Sudbury. Although Daisy never became a concert performer, Oscar has always had the highest regard for his sister's playing. In a 1982 interview, he called her "a great pianist."

The youngest of the siblings, May, also became a piano teacher. Later she worked for Oscar as his personal secretary, a job that was helpful for Oscar and gave May some financial security.

★ ★ ★

During the time that Oscar was at the Alberta Lounge, he made several more recordings with his trio for the Victor label. The first one, in December 1947, was called "Oscar's Boogie." Even then, Oscar had not entirely put boogie-woogie behind him. Then just over a year later, Oscar recorded Dizzy Gillespie's "Oop-Bop-Sha-Bam," an interesting tune for several reasons.

For one, "Oop-Bop-Sha-Bam" is Oscar's first recording as a singer. Oscar's voice is light and pleasant and sounds a lot like Nat Cole's. Oscar would sing on several more recordings over the next few years, but then he stopped singing for quite a while, at least on his records. The story is that Nat Cole went to hear Oscar play one night — by then they were friends — and after the show he went backstage and made Oscar a proposal. Cole said he would stop playing the piano if Oscar would stop singing. The two men agreed. Oscar didn't sing again on records until he put out an album in tribute to Nat Cole, the year after Cole's death.

"Oop-Bop-Sha-Bam" shows how much Oscar had grown as a player since his first recordings in 1945. Dizzy Gillespie's tune is a classic example of bebop. It features a complicated melody line full of twists and turns, and Oscar handles it with confidence and assurance. He had been listening closely to this new jazz style. Now he was proving he could play it as well as any other style he undertook to learn.

Oscar playing with his father, Daniel Peterson. Daniel saw music as the key to a brighter future for his children.

(Canadian Pacific Railway Archives. Image no. A21396)

Oscar accompanying his brother Chuck. Despite losing his forearm in an accident, Chuck went on to have a career as a professional trumpet player.
(Canadian Pacific Railway Archives. Image no. A21399)

By the time Oscar was in his mid-teens, he was getting considerable attention for his piano virtuosity and had become the star attraction of the Johnny Holmes Orchestra, Montreal's leading swing band.
(Canadian Pacific Railway Archives. Image no. A21392)

Oscar and his family pose for a photographer from the Canadian Pacific Railway, his father's employer. From left to right are Chuck, Oscar, Daniel, Olive, May and Daisy.

(Canadian Pacific Railway Archives. Image no. A21395)

Johnny Holmes, the Montreal bandleader, became Oscar's mentor, teaching him to play with more sensitivity and refinement. They met regularly to listen to records and go through the band's music.

(Johnny Holmes Collection, Concordia University Archives)

Oscar joined the Johnny Holmes Orchestra in 1942, when he was just seventeen. As the only black member of the band, he encountered discrimination from some people who were not prepared to see black and white musicians on stage together.

(Johnny Holmes Collection, Concordia University Archives)

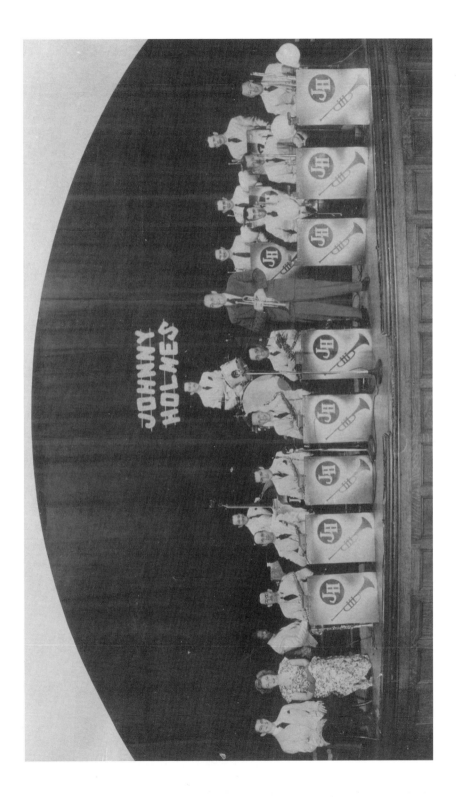

The young Oscar Peterson performing at a community center in Toronto in 1946, surrounded by a group of admiring fans. By this time Oscar was well known across Canada.

From 1947 to 1949, Oscar led this trio (with Austin Roberts on bass and Clarence Jones on drums) at the Alberta Lounge in Montreal. Oscar's big break came when promoter Norman Granz heard a live radio broadcast of the trio and invited Oscar to make a guest appearance with Jazz at the Philharmonic (JATP), Granz's company of jazz greats.

(Salmon Studios, Montreal. Photo from the Oscar Peterson fonds, Music Division, National Library of Canada)

Oscar with his older sister, Daisy, working on a musical problem. Daisy, an accomplished pianist, was Oscar's first music teacher. She went on to become one of Montreal's finest piano teachers.

(Photo from the Elitha Peterson Productions fonds, Music Division, National Library of Canada)

One of the great trios in jazz. Oscar with Ray Brown (bass) and Herb Ellis (guitar) at a club in Toronto in the mid-1950s. (Sun Media Corporation)

Jazz at the Philharmonic (JATP), the company made up of some of the best jazz musicians in America, performed in concert halls and clubs around the world. Here JATP is greeted by enthusiastic fans on its arrival in Japan.

(Photo from the Oscar Peterson fonds, Music Division, National Library of Canada)

On August 8, 1956, Oscar, Ray Brown and Herb Ellis performed at the Stratford Shakespearean Festival in Ontario, Canada. The recording of that concert is still regarded as one of the trio's finest.
(Courtesy of Universal Music Canada. From the Recorded Sound and Video Collection of the National Library of Canada)

After Herb Ellis left the trio, Oscar hired Ed Thigpen, a drummer known for his mastery with brushes. Oscar has described Ed's tenure with the trio as "six years of unbelievable music."
(André Le Coz for CBC. From the Recorded Sound and Video Collection of the National Library of Canada)

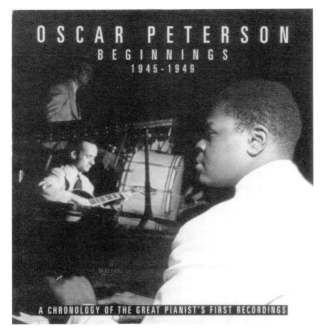

The cover from a CD reissue of Oscar's earliest recordings. Although his speed and technical assurance is remarkable for a musician barely out of his teens, Oscar is still focused on boogie-woogie and is a few years away from reaching his mature style.
(Courtesy of BMG Music Canada. From the Recorded Sound and Video Collection of the National Library of Canada)

Ella Fitzgerald, the great jazz vocalist, was a regular member of Norman Granz's JATP. She and Oscar played and recorded together frequently over the years, and had a deep respect for each other's ability.
(Photo from the Oscar Peterson fonds, Music Division, National Library of Canada)

Oscar and his wife Lil at home with their five children in 1959. From left to right are Norman, Oscar Jr., Gay, Sharon and Lynn.

Oscar with hands raised, coaching a student.
(Ehricht, Horst/National Archives of Canada/PA-206569)

Oscar at a blackboard.
(Ehricht, Horst/National Archives of Canada/PA-206568)

Oscar at the Advanced School of Contemporary Music (ASCM).
(Ehricht, Horst/National Archives of Canada/PA-206567)

Oscar giving a private lesson to a young pianist.
(Ehricht, Horst/National Archives of Canada/PA-206566)

Oscar at his Toronto home in the early 1980s, surrounded by his impressive collection of synthesizers and recording equipment. He also developed a serious interest in photography and carried a portable darkroom with him when he was on the road.

A 1984 portrait of a relaxed Oscar Peterson. Just months earlier he had been promoted to Companion of the Order of Canada, the highest honor that can be bestowed on a Canadian citizen.

(From Companions of the Order of Canada. Palmer, Harry/National Archives of Canada/PA-182399)

Oscar in November, 1991, presiding over his first convocation as chancellor of York University. (Courtesy of York University)

Oscar was learning quickly that to survive as a black musician at that time, he had to be able to deal with all kinds of people. Every year, a man would come up from Georgia to hear him and his trio at the Alberta Lounge. One night he came up to the bandstand to meet Oscar. Without thinking, Oscar reached out to shake the man's hand. The man pulled back his hand, saying, "I love your playing, but I could never shake hands with a nigger."

Some players found the abuse and prejudice too much to endure, and they turned to destructive things like alcohol and drugs. Oscar never did. He was determined not to let narrow-minded and bigoted fools keep him from realizing his goal.

By 1949, it was becoming clear that there simply were not enough playing opportunities to keep him in Canada forever. The real pulse of jazz was in the big American cities. Oscar began to plan his next move, to travel to the States and do some gigs there.

He was just too good a pianist and too determined a person to be kept off the international stage for much longer. As it happened, though, just at that time a new person appeared in his life. This person took the planning and decision-making out of Oscar's hands and into his own. He quickly became Oscar's advisor, manager, record producer and very close friend. His name was Norman Granz.

Count Basie (1904–1984)

When William Basie was a child, he would watch his mother as she worked, washing and ironing for wealthy families in their small New Jersey town. He promised her that when he grew up she would no longer have to be a laundress, that he would "take care of her and buy her beautiful things and also be somebody that she would be proud of."

Basie struggled at school, but he had a gift for picking out ragtime melodies on the family piano. When he was a young man he moved to New York, where he learned Harlem stride piano technique from the leading players in that style, including James P. Johnson and Fats Waller. Before long he was performing on the black vaudeville circuits as a solo pianist, accompanist and musical director.

In 1927, while he was in Kansas City, Basie developed spinal meningitis and almost died. When he recovered he decided to stay in K.C., which in those days was a major center for the emerging jazz swing style. Soon he was a leading player in the new style. It was in Kansas City that he also decided to give himself a new name. Duke Ellington, King Oliver and Earl Hines were already famous players, so William Basie decided a noble name would suit him, too. He had business cards that read: "COUNT BASIE. Beware the Count is Here."

By 1935 Count Basie had organized a new band, the Barons of Rhythm, which performed in Kansas City and on radio broadcasts and records. By 1938 the Barons of Rhythm had become the Count Basie Orchestra, which established itself as one of the top big bands of the swing era. Many of the leading jazz musicians of the day spent time with the orchestra, including Lester Young and vocalists Jimmy Rushing and Billie Holiday.

Basie made New York his orchestra's home base, but he brought along many of the features of Kansas City style jazz. Riffs — repeated figures played by the brass and saxophone sections — often provided the background for the soloists, and were a contrast to the more complicated written arrangements of Duke Ellington's orchestra. Basie's brilliant rhythm section helped to bring a four-beat pulse (playing four beats to the bar rather than two) into common practice in jazz performance.

Count Basie was an accomplished ragtime and stride pianist, but he chose to play in a simple, sparse style that blended in well with the sound of his orchestra. He had a completely different style from Oscar Peterson, and yet they had a deep respect for each other's playing, and they performed and recorded together many times. Oscar called Basie "an idol and mentor of mine," and in his autobiography, Basie described the experience of hearing Oscar play: "I just sit there in the wings just looking and listening, because what he does is really incredible… it's impossible for anybody to sit down at the piano and play and think that fast."

Basie remained leader of his orchestra until his death, but the Count Basie Orchestra continues to perform, providing an important link to the swing era.

6

Debut at Carnegie Hall

Norman Granz was a striking-looking man — tall and handsome, with thick bushy eyebrows that curled upwards. He spoke his mind about many things, but especially about jazz, the music he loved so much. Not everyone loved Norman Granz, but most would agree that he made important contributions to how jazz was seen and heard in America. Many jazz musicians benefited directly from the changes he brought about — perhaps no one more than Oscar Peterson.

Granz was born in Los Angeles in 1918, but soon his family moved to Long Beach, California, where his father owned a department store. There were few other Jewish families in Long Beach, so Granz grew up playing with kids of all different ent colors and ethnic backgrounds.

World War Two was raging, and Granz knew he would soon be called up to serve in the army. In the meantime, he decided to go to New York and have some fun. Before long, he found himself on 52nd Street, home to some of the best jazz in the world. As he wandered from club to club, listening to one great jazz band after another, he knew he had found the world he wanted to be part of.

He decided to become a jazz promoter, someone who arranges club and concert dates for musicians and keeps a percentage of the profits. He went back to Los Angeles and began to book jam sessions at a nightclub called the Trouville Club. Through this he got to know musicians such as Count Basie and Nat Cole. After he was drafted, the army found out that Granz had formed friendships with some of the black enlisted men. In the deeply segregated world of the United States military, Granz's actions were frowned upon. His application for officer's training was turned down, and in 1943 he was discharged from the army. He returned to Los Angeles, where he went right back to booking jazz.

In most American and Canadian cities at that time, clubs and dance halls barred blacks from the audience. That left jazz musicians, most of whom were black, playing mainly for white people. One time Granz saw Billie Holiday, the great jazz singer, crying at the Trouville Club, because the management wouldn't let her black friends in to hear her sing.

Norman Granz saw this, and other incidents like it, and he decided that he would do whatever he could to break down the racism and segregation that existed in the jazz world. He knew there was a union rule that clubs had to give their regular musicians one night off every week. This rule forced clubs to close their doors for that night. Granz approached Billy Berg, a successful club owner in Los Angeles, with the idea of setting up jam sessions on the club's so-called "dark night." Granz would supply the musicians, and the club owner would not lose a night's business.

But Granz insisted on certain conditions. Jam sessions were usually informal gatherings of musicians playing without an audience and without pay. Granz wanted to attract paying customers for his sessions, and so he decided to hire top musicians and advertise the sessions.

At that time most jazz clubs had dance floors for the customers. Granz believed that the jazz he was promoting was better suited for listening, not dancing. He placed tables on the dance floor, so the audience would have to sit and listen to the musicians. Finally, he insisted that the clubs be open to black patrons as well as white.

Berg agreed to Granz's conditions, and before long the best players in town were playing in Norman Granz's jam sessions. Nat Cole was the regular pianist, and members of Duke Ellington's and Jimmie Lunceford's bands were often available. The great saxophone player, Lester Young, and his brother, Lee Young, a drummer, were also regulars.

The jam sessions were a roaring success. Soon other owners wanted to book Granz's sessions for their "dark nights." Granz went from club to club with his sessions, hiring musicians as they were available.

To many of the black players, Norman Granz was an odd fellow — a strange white kid with a sharp tongue who liked hanging around musicians. He dressed like a rich college student, with his sloppy open collar and sweaters and brown-and-white saddle shoes. He never touched alcohol, but drank malted milkshakes instead. Norman might have seemed strange to the musicians, but they couldn't argue with his success, or with the respect and love he showed to them and their music.

One Sunday afternoon in July 1944, Granz put on a jazz concert at the Philharmonic Auditorium in Los Angeles, booking several well-known musicians for the event. The auditorium was filled with young fans who yelled and whistled their approval for everything they heard. The concert was a smash hit. For the rest of that year, Granz scheduled monthly concerts at the Philharmonic.

As popular as his jam sessions and concerts had been,

Norman Granz knew that black musicians faced the reality of segregation each time they went on the road to play. In those days, being black in the United States meant that you were only allowed into certain restrooms or hotels or restaurants. Well into the 1960s, businesses posted signs in their windows that said "White Only." If you were black, you looked for the signs that said "For Colored." Even drinking fountains had signs posted above them saying "White" or "Colored."

Norman Granz decided to use Jazz at the Philharmonic (JATP) to break into segregated hotels, restaurants and concert halls in the United States. He would take some of the musicians — both black and white — from his JATP concerts and go on the road. In a brilliant stroke of courage, Jazz at the Philharmonic became a traveling showcase for some of the best in jazz.

In 1945, Granz took his troupe on a tour of the West Coast. It was in Victoria, British Columbia, that he heard a young pianist on a jukebox, playing some boogie-woogie. The pianist was Oscar Peterson.

Granz's first tour was not very successful financially. He used up all his savings to pay for his musicians' travel expenses. But he was not about to let a minor setback like that slow him down. He decided to record some of his live concerts and try to sell them to record companies.

No one had ever recorded a live jazz performance before — a performance from a concert hall or club rather than from the studio. Many people in the recording business thought that Norman Granz was crazy for trying. In a live recording there could be problems caused by crowd noise and poor acoustics of the hall or club. But Granz was not deterred. He felt that a live recording offered a level of excitement and immediacy that a studio record could not.

Granz went off to New York with a pile of JATP recordings under his arm, in search of a buyer. He met with Moses Asch of Asch Records, and the men came to an agreement. Asch put out the records as Volume One of *Jazz at the Philharmonic*. Jazz fans rushed to buy the records, which became very popular. The first recording ever made of a live jazz concert launched Norman Granz's career as one of the most successful record producers in the history of jazz.

★ ★ ★

The story of how Norman Granz first heard Oscar Peterson — told by Granz himself and backed up by Oscar — has been repeated so often it is almost a legend in jazz circles. Legends are important because they are good stories, not because everything in them is true. Although Granz had heard Oscar on a jukebox in Victoria in 1945, he liked to tell a more dramatic story of hearing him for the first time in 1949.

Granz said that he was in a taxi, on his way to the airport in Montreal, when some jazz came on the car radio. He asked the driver what station they were listening to, because he wanted to call up the station and find out who was playing such great piano. The driver told him they were listening to a live broadcast from the Alberta Lounge, and that the pianist was Oscar Peterson. Granz told the driver to turn around and take him to the Alberta Lounge.

Norman Granz might have embellished his story somewhat, but there is little doubt as to what happened next. He sat and listened to Oscar and his trio, and when the band took a break, he went over to talk to him. He told Oscar he had a good shot at doing well in the U.S. jazz market. He said that Oscar would stand out as being different from many of the other pianists of his time, both because he was Canadian and because of his awesome technique and mastery of many piano styles.

Granz told Oscar he liked introducing surprise guests from the audience at his JATP concerts, usually right after the intermission. He had a concert scheduled for September at Carnegie Hall in New York City. Why not come down to New York with him, Granz suggested, and he would introduce Oscar from the audience to come up and play?

Oscar hesitated. It's not that he didn't want to go to the States. He had in fact been thinking about it for quite some time. But New York City was the heartbeat of jazz in America, and Carnegie Hall was one of the most famous concert halls in the entire world. Oscar told Granz he had been hoping to start out a little smaller, to work his way up.

Granz had an answer for that. He said to Oscar, "Take your best shot, you'll know in one shot. You won't have to dilly-dally. If you make it, you'll know it. If you don't make it, you'll know that too." Oscar agreed to go to New York.

Among the musicians in Granz's JATP troupe at that time was a young bass player named Ray Brown. He and Oscar already knew each other a little bit, because Brown would stop by the Alberta Lounge when he was in Montreal on tour with JATP. But Oscar had been paying attention to Ray Brown long before that. Brown was the bassist Oscar had listened to in high school — the bassist he declared would be in his own trio one day. Now Brown was going to accompany Oscar in his debut at Carnegie Hall.

Granz had originally planned for Oscar to be backed by bass and drums. Buddy Rich, the drummer with JATP at that time, was a fiery player who put his heart and soul into each performance. Rich usually played a long drum solo just before the intermission, and sometimes he wore himself out with the effort. That is what happened on September 18, 1949. Rich came back to the dressing room at intermission, just as Granz was preparing to introduce Oscar, and said that he was too tired to go right back on stage. That left Oscar and Ray Brown to perform as a duo.

They played "Tenderly," a popular jazz standard of the day. By the end of the performance, the audience was screaming and cheering. Norman Granz gave Oscar the signal to stay on stage and play some more.

Oscar got rave reviews for his debut at Carnegie Hall. "A Montreal citizen, Oscar Peterson, stopped the Norman Granz Jazz at the Phil concert dead cold in its tracks here last month," wrote Michael Levin in *Down Beat* magazine. Levin mentioned Oscar's flashy right hand and his good sense of harmonic development. He added that not only did Oscar have good ideas — here Levin was referring to the melodies and harmonies Oscar was creating as he improvised — but that Oscar was able to give them "a rhythmic punch and drive which has been all too lacking in too many of the younger pianists."

A British jazz writer, Richard Palmer, said that Oscar's debut at Carnegie Hall was especially dramatic because American jazz fans had not heard much about Oscar before then. "He burst upon the American scene," Palmer said, "with the impact of a new planet."

After the concert, Oscar went back to Montreal. Granz felt that they had done what they set out to do, which was to introduce Oscar to the U.S. jazz market. He encouraged Oscar to "cool it" for a while, to keep working on his music and think about which direction he wanted to take next. Then they would get together and talk things over.

Oscar did not return to the States until the following fall, when he joined JATP for his first full tour. In the meantime, he kept busy in Montreal, playing and preparing for his future career. But Oscar also had other things on his mind. He and Lil had become parents for the first time in 1948, when their daughter Lynn was born. The next year they had another daughter, Sharon.

By now Lil must have realized that her husband's career would be taking him away from home for long periods of time, and that the responsibility of raising the children would fall mainly on her shoulders. As much as Oscar loved Lil and his children, in some ways his music would always come first. He had a special gift, and he had every intention of using that gift to go as far as he could.

Besides, Oscar himself grew up in a home where the father and breadwinner of the family was often away because of his work. Perhaps he did not think it was strange that he too would spend much of his time on the road. Then there were the practical reasons for joining JATP. Norman Granz paid his musicians better than almost anyone else in the music business. By going where his career took him, Oscar would be making more money than he could ever imagine earning if he stayed in Canada. The better he did, he reasoned, the more opportunities he could offer to his children.

In 1950, Oscar returned to the States to join Jazz at the Philharmonic on tour. He would always keep a home in Canada, but except for one brief period in the early 1960s, he would spend the next forty years as a resident of the world. At the age of twenty-five, he was already Canada's best-known jazz musician. Soon he would be one of the most recognized and respected jazz pianists anywhere.

7

A Taste of
Jim Crow

Oscar Peterson did indeed embark on an adventure when he
joined Norman Granz's Jazz at the Philharmonic. The adventure was not all fun and games, though, especially in the
beginning.

Oscar worried about how the other musicians would react
to him, the kid from Canada with the big buildup. In Montreal
he had been the young prodigy, supported by a cast of able but
less gifted performers. Now he was in the big leagues, surrounded by some of the most talented and experienced jazz
stars of his time. There was Ella Fitzgerald, the great jazz
singer; Roy Eldridge on trumpet; Lester Young, Ben Webster
and Illinois Jacquet on saxophone; drummers Buddy Rich and
Gene Krupa; bassist Ray Brown, among many others.
Suddenly Oscar found himself playing with the very musicians whose recordings he had been listening to for years.

The first tour was rough, as Oscar himself would later
admit. His usual self-confidence abandoned him, and he
played cautiously, afraid to make mistakes or draw the criticism of the other musicians.

As if that weren't enough, Oscar was also getting his first taste of Jim Crow, the laws that enforced segregation throughout the southern United States. As much as he had encountered prejudice and discrimination growing up in Canada, nothing could prepare him for the treatment that he and the other black musicians received as they toured through the South. There, violence and brutality against blacks and other minorities went way beyond being asked to go somewhere else, or being treated with disrespect. In some places, if you were black and stood up for your rights, you were risking your life.

In a *Maclean's* interview from that period, Oscar said, "Travelling in the South, it feels like you're not just in another world, you're on some other planet." The Jim Crow laws were apparent everywhere the musicians went. They would drive up to a restaurant, and a sign would stare them in the face, telling them that "colored" were not allowed. The white musicians would have to bring food out to the car so their black friends could eat. Oscar loved to eat, but often, after one of these experiences, he didn't have much of an appetite.

Sometimes Norman Granz hired a bus for the troupe, when they were going from one small town or city to the next. The bus would stop in front of a hotel where the white players were going to stay, and Oscar would look out at the big, fancy building with its grand windows. He would watch the faces of the doormen as they caught sight of the black musicians on the bus, and he knew they were thinking, "They're not planning to come in here." Oscar was learning the rules of the South. If you were black, you stayed away from places where you were not wanted, or you were asking for trouble.

Yet these same musicians were drawing sell-out crowds to their concerts every night, bringing down the house with their wonderful music. Within a few years, members of Granz's troupe were among the highest-paid and most recorded jazz musicians in the business.

For the musicians, though, no measure of financial success could make up for the pain and humiliation they were forced to endure. To his enormous credit, Norman Granz saw this, and he began to push hard for change. Just as he had done in his early JATP jam sessions in Los Angeles, he made promoters sign contracts that forced them to admit both blacks and whites to the concerts.

Granz meant business. When he found out that the promoters of a concert in New Orleans were planning to have segregated seating, he canceled the concert. At the same time, he began booking the entire troupe into the best hotels, even those that had previously barred blacks. And more than once, Granz chartered a plane to get his musicians out of southern towns that seemed especially dangerous.

Over the years, Granz and his troupe had many ugly confrontations with racist white Southerners, including southern police, who were well known for their brutality against blacks and other minorities. One time the troupe was at an airport in Texas, and Granz directed Ella Fitzgerald toward a cab. A big southern police officer came up to them, his large gun in full view, and said that she was not getting in that cab. Granz calmly replied, "She has a right to get in that cab — she's getting in that cab." The officer pulled out the gun and pushed it against Granz's stomach, saying, "Ain't one of these niggers getting in any of these cabs. If they do, I'm gonna kill you."

Ella Fitzgerald was shaking with fear, but Granz insisted that she get in the car, that the officer was not going to do anything. Granz was right. The officer just stood there, but not before telling Granz that he hated him "worse than I hate these niggers." In his eyes, Granz was the scum of the earth

— "a nigger lover," to use the phrase of the southern bigots. Oscar can still remember the look of helpless rage on the policeman's face when he realized that Granz was getting the upper hand.

Another time Oscar was driving in the South with bassist Ray Brown. He was taking his turn at the wheel while Brown took a nap, and he stopped at a diner for cigarettes. A couple of policemen were in the diner, and they watched as Oscar went up to the cash and pulled out a twenty-dollar bill to pay for the cigarettes.

The man behind the counter looked at Oscar. He saw a well-dressed black man carrying a lot of money for those days, and his prejudices came rushing to the surface. "Where did you get twenty dollars, boy?" he asked Oscar. Oscar replied that he had earned it. The man gave him the cigarettes but threw his change on the floor.

One of the officers stepped toward Oscar, his hand on his gun. "Pick it up, boy," he said. In Montreal, Oscar had stood up to the policeman who tried to arrest him, but this was different. He was in the South, and he knew that this officer would not hesitate to use his gun. Without saying a word, Oscar picked up his change and left the diner. He was furious. When he got back to the car he tried to persuade Ray Brown to wait with him until the policemen had left, so that he could go back after the man at the counter.

Ray Brown was American, and he had seen much more of southern racism than Oscar had. He knew when bravery crossed the line into stupidity, and finally he convinced Oscar to drive away.

The musicians themselves were often way ahead of their society when it came to racial issues. It was not that they were better or wiser than anyone else, or that they all came from homes where tolerance and understanding were taught. They simply knew that being able to play well had nothing to do with the color of your skin. They would play together because of their mutual respect and admiration. And often they would see that the supposed differences between them weren't nearly as great as they were made out to be.

Some of the braver musicians tried to break down the barriers that society had put up. The struggle was long and painful, and change did not come overnight. Before 1937, jazz was strictly segregated in the United States. Not only were the audiences not allowed to mix, but black and white musicians could only play together in the after-hours clubs, where the players went to jam after they were through with their regular gigs.

Then, in 1937, Benny Carter, the great black saxophone and trumpet player, hired white and black musicians for a band he was leading in Holland, a country known for its racial tolerance.

Benny Goodman, the Jewish bandleader and clarinetist, followed Carter's example. He hired some outstanding black musicians for his band, including Teddy Wilson, one of the pianists Oscar most admired. Other white bandleaders, including Artie Shaw and Tommy Dorsey, all hired black musicians. Some of the black bandleaders did the same in reverse. The bebop trumpeter, Dizzy Gillespie, hired musicians based on their abilities rather than their color. Count Basie hired Buddy Rich, the drummer who also played with JATP.

Slowly but surely, the barriers came down. Through the efforts of the musicians themselves, and the courage and determination of Norman Granz and others, society began to accept integration on the bandstand and in the audiences.

★ ★ ★

By the end of his second tour in 1951, Oscar had shaken off his rookie nerves. His self-confidence had returned, and he felt that the other musicians were showing that they had confidence in him as well. Oscar's competitive nature served him well in this situation. He had listened carefully to the big players on the jazz scene, and he was sure he would be able to compete on their level.

Oscar was certainly not alone in thinking of jazz performance as a kind of competition. There was a long tradition of "cutting contests," where musicians would jam for hours, trying to outplay one another. Speed, technical ability and interesting and creative solos were the goals of every musician in a cutting contest. Musicians would take turns on stage, playing chorus after chorus, until the so-called winner was left standing. Most jazz musicians of Oscar's era had considerable experience with these contests.

By and large, though, competition in the jazz world was friendly. Ella Fitzgerald said that one of the reasons JATP was so successful was because the musicians were there for each other. Their main goal was to put on a great show, and to do that they had to work together. Oscar believed that competition made the musicians work harder and gave them the extra push they needed to play their best.

And in the bassist Ray Brown, Oscar found someone who could match his drive and competitive spirit. From the moment they took the stage together at Oscar's Carnegie Hall debut, they hit it off both personally and musically.

Bass players have a crucial role in any jazz band. They are responsible for keeping a steady tempo and for providing the harmonic foundation, or structure, of the music. Ray Brown once said that the greatest assets a bass player can have are good time, good intonation (the ability to play the instrument in tune), and a big sound. Brown had all of these in abundance.

From the moment Oscar joined JATP, he and Ray Brown were practically inseparable. According to Ben Webster, one of the saxophonists who toured with them, Oscar and Ray were always working on their music, going over and over something until they got it right. Webster said that he never saw anyone as keen on music as Oscar and Ray. Even when the curtain went down for the intermission, the two of them would stay right there rehearsing until the concert began again.

Ray credited Oscar with much of his musical development. He said that Oscar always threw a little more at him than he thought he could handle, so that he was always being challenged to improve, to reach new heights. Because the bass is a large, awkward instrument, fast scales or rapid position changes are hard to manage. Oscar would say to Ray, "Is this possible on the instrument?" More often than not, Ray Brown would find a way.

Oscar once said, "Ray has an insatiable desire — insatiable, absolutely insatiable — to find the right note at the right time." Many players will practice something until they come up with the notes they are looking for, and then they are satisfied. Ray Brown was only satisfied that time around. The next time they played the tune, Oscar would see Ray concentrating as he approached the same spot, and then he would play something else that would work better.

When JATP was not touring, Norman Granz got Oscar and Ray steady work as a duo, booking them into clubs throughout the States and Canada. In May 1951, they had a week's engagement in Hamilton, Ontario, in the Hunting Room of the Fischer Hotel.

At some point in the week, Ray Brown realized he needed

a haircut. For a traveling black musician in those days, finding a barber was complicated. In the early fifties, most barber shops in North America were segregated, if not by law then by practice. White people went to white barbers, and blacks went to black barbers.

Ray Brown could not find a black barber in Hamilton, but he did find a barber shop and decided to go in. The white owner, Glenn McQuaid, gave him a haircut. Because he had had no trouble, Ray recommended the place to Oscar, who went the next day. This time Glenn McQuaid was not there, and another barber told Oscar that the shop was closed. When Oscar came back later, he was again told the shop was closed, even though at that moment a white customer was sitting down to have his hair cut.

Oscar called the police. They advised him to tell the barber that he would call the crown attorney to complain if the barber would not cut his hair. Once again Oscar returned to the shop, and once again the barber refused.

Oscar called Lloyd Fischer, the owner of the hotel where he and Ray were playing, and Fischer called the crown attorney's office. The story made the Hamilton *Spectator* on May 5, 1951. Oscar told the paper that it had been his boast on United States tours "that Jim Crow did not live in Canada — it was a great country." He added, "But when something like this happens to you, it almost makes you feel that you are not a man. It hurt to watch that man walk past me and get served. I have three little girls. And it sort of made me wonder what kind of world it will be when they grow up."

The story was widely reported across Canada. On May 7, the owner, Glenn McQuaid, told the newspaper that he had cut the hair of "Mr. Peterson's companion," and he would have cut Oscar's hair if he had been there. Then he insisted that he was "the only man in the shop qualified to cut a negro's hair." He said that he had learned this skill many years before, and that without knowing the correct way to do it, a barber would just break combs. "I have cut negroes' hair in the past in my shop," he added, "and I will continue to do so in the future. That is not discrimination." Then McQuaid said that Oscar went to the police instead of being a "gentleman and going elsewhere." In other words, Oscar's mistake was to stand up for his rights.

The mayor of Hamilton, Lloyd D. Jackson, jumped into the fray. He told the *Spectator*, "I hate to see the stinking thing called racial intolerance raising its head in the city. I am ashamed to think it would happen here. I never dreamed anyone would refuse to cut the hair of a negro."

People began to picket McQuaid's shop, protesting the treatment Oscar had received. McQuaid went to the police, complaining that the pickets were preventing people from entering his shop. Eventually the uproar died down, but not before some changes were put in place. The city of Hamilton voted that business licenses would include in writing a statement forbidding discrimination in any form. Glenn McQuaid apologized to Hamilton's Board of Control, and the board let him off the hook, saying that "Mr. McQuaid did not merit punishment as he was absent when the incident took place."

Oscar Peterson had simply wanted to have a haircut, but in the end, he got many people in Hamilton and other parts of Canada talking about prejudice.

★ ★ ★

By 1952, Oscar's career was really starting to take off. He and Ray Brown continued to perform both as a duo and as part of Granz's larger ensemble, and by now they had made several more recordings together, all under Granz's direction.

Still, Norman Granz was not satisfied. As successful as the duo of Oscar and Ray had been, Granz was convinced that they would do even better if they added a third player to the mix. Oscar had worked with different trio combinations since the mid-forties, mostly with musicians from the Montreal area. Now, under Granz's direction, Oscar and Ray began trying out different players, searching for the right fit.

They played briefly with drummer Charlie Smith. Then they decided to try the combination of instruments Nat Cole had used: piano, bass and guitar. The first two guitarists they tried stayed only for a short time. Then Ray Brown heard a band called the Soft Winds, a trio consisting of Lou Carter on piano, John Frigo on bass and Herb Ellis on guitar. Ray told Oscar about the band, and Oscar went to hear them himself. When Oscar heard Herb Ellis, he knew he had found what he was looking for. He approached Ellis and offered him a job, and Ellis accepted. As simply as that, one of the great jazz trios of all time was born.

Ray Brown (1926–2002)

Ray Brown began to play the bass when he was in junior high school in Pittsburgh. He used an instrument owned by the school, and he would take it home on weekends to practice. Before long he was playing gigs. When school officials found out that he was using their instrument to make money, they forbade him to take the bass home. Ray's father, convinced of Ray's devotion to his music, saved up money to buy his son a bass.

After Ray graduated from high school he played in territory bands — touring bands that played through the mid-western United States. In 1945, when he was just nineteen, he went to New York and immersed himself in the new jazz style of the day, bebop. Dizzy Gillespie and Charlie Parker, two of the leading figures of bebop, invited him to rehearse with their quintet. Later he toured with Gillespie and played on several bebop recordings.

From 1947, Ray Brown was a regular member of Jazz at the Philharmonic, but it was his work with Oscar Peterson that earned him recognition as one of the leading bassists in jazz. Oscar once said that Ray had a talent that was "almost ethereal." He explained that Ray had such a strong sense of the sound he wanted to get from a bass that he could make even an inferior instrument sound great.

After he left the Oscar Peterson Trio in 1966, Ray Brown continued to play and record with many other jazz greats, including Duke Ellington, Jimmie Rowles, Monty Alexander and Cedar Walton. In the mid-nineties he made two albums called *Some of my Best Friends are... the Piano Players*, and *Some of my Best Friends are ... the Sax*

Players, bringing together several of his favorite players for the sessions, including his old friend, Oscar Peterson. He continued to perform right up to his death in 2002, leaving behind a legacy as one of the great jazz bassists of all time.

8

Oscar, Ray and Herb

When Herb Ellis joined the Oscar Peterson Trio in 1954, Oscar received hate letters from both blacks and whites, criticizing him for having an integrated band. Oscar had no time for such foolishness. He hired Herb Ellis because he was an excellent guitarist, and because the two of them got along, right off the bat.

And something special happened when Herb joined the band. As close as Oscar and Ray had been as a duo, Herb fit in like the missing piece of a puzzle. He came from a very different background than his bandmates, but music stripped away their differences and left what Oscar called a "close-knit unit."

The first thing Oscar noticed about Herb Ellis was his remarkable sense of time. Oscar's own time was superb, and the players he most admired had that same driving, swinging quality to their playing. Herb stayed with the Oscar Peterson Trio until 1958. For all three members of the band, those years were special, a time when they would play some of the best music of their careers and form a closeness with one another that would last a lifetime.

Perhaps the key to their success, though, was their shared vision of what it takes to make a great band. For as talented as Oscar, Ray and Herb were as individuals, they knew that did not necessarily mean they would play well together. They were aiming for a level of communication as a group that only the best bands are able to achieve — a communication in which the musicians speak to each other through their instruments.

That level of communication does not happen overnight. As Ray Brown said, "If you want to be that good playing jazz, you have to work at it all the time." Ray and Herb had an extra incentive to rehearse as much as they did. Oscar was a demanding leader who did not hesitate to show his displeasure if his bandmates failed to deliver what he expected.

To keep up with him, Ray and Herb practiced for long stretches each day, just the two of them. They roomed together when the band was on the road, and they had a routine. In the morning they played golf, and then in the afternoon they got together to play. Like all good jazz musicians, they were striving to keep their playing fresh and interesting. They would play a tune they had played many times before and practice harmonic substitutions — different ways of combining chords over a given melody. In this way they were sharpening their ears and their minds, preparing themselves for whatever Oscar might throw at them in the club that night. After their session they would shower, take a nap, have dinner, and go off to the gig.

When good musicians work that hard, the results can be spectacular. Oscar would later say that this band had "three people that were really involved in playing for one another. I don't think just Herbie and Ray were involved in playing for me, which they did, beautifully; it was also the way Ray made me come up with the best possible background for Herbie...

And the same thing would have to be said when Herbie and I played for Ray."

Sometimes there are problems when two chording instruments play at the same time. The notes selected by the guitarist and pianist can clash with each other, or the combination of chords can sound muddy. With Oscar and Herb, this almost never happened. They had learned to listen to each other so well that each could usually anticipate the direction the other was going, even when they were improvising.

Musicians talk about playing in the groove, that sweet spot where they lock in with one another as if they are playing with one common stream of energy. Oscar simply called it the "lock-down." When the trio had "the lock-down going," Oscar said, "it was a unit that nobody could interfere with."

In Oscar's earlier trios, he took center stage and the other musicians were there in a supporting role. Now with Ray Brown and Herb Ellis, the trio was much more an equal partnership, with all three musicians having the opportunity to solo and stretch out.

The number and variety of tunes in the trio's repertoire was astonishing. They played originals, bebop tunes, jazz classics, show tunes and the blues. According to Ray Brown, Oscar composed some hard music, but he didn't write it down. He would teach it to Ray and Herb by ear and expect them to memorize it. Then Oscar might come in the next night and ask them to play the same arrangement, but this time in another key.

Oscar demanded a great deal of Ray and Herb, but no more than he demanded of himself. He seemed driven to prove that he was the best piano player and had the best band around. Perhaps without even knowing it, he was still trying to please his father.

Oscar said in a 1951 interview that his father was still his harshest critic. "He's never come out and said he's liked anything I've done. Sometimes, after hearing me play he'll say, 'You're not gonna go up and get your pay for that.'" But another time Oscar told the story of the night Daniel Peterson came out to the club to hear him play. The crowd was really into the music that night, and several times there were bursts of enthusiastic applause. Oscar happened to look out into the audience and caught the expression on his father's face. It was an expression of pride mixed with relief, as if his father was finally able to say, "Well, he's escaped the railroad, that's for sure."

That look from his father spurred Oscar on. Perhaps it made him demand even more of himself and of those around him. One thing is certain. Oscar's drive to succeed made him very competitive. There were several other piano players and groups making more money than Oscar and his trio, and Oscar was not happy about it. He was convinced that his band deserved to make as much as any of them. In his mind, his only solution was to take up the challenge, to "wipe every piano player around," as he put it, in order to get the recognition he deserved.

One time the trio was opening for the Count Basie Orchestra. Oscar told Herb and Ray that they were outnumbered, but they were every bit as good a band as Basie's. Ray Brown said, "You understand, they were our closest friends in the world, but on the bandstand, Oscar takes no prisoners."

Sometimes Oscar's demand for perfection was too much for Ray and Herb. After one gig Oscar left the bandstand looking very dissatisfied. Ray saw this and confronted Oscar. "Just what do you expect of this group?" he asked. Oscar replied, "Only a little music." Later on Oscar listened to a recording of that evening's performance and realized that the band had played quite well. He called Ray Brown to tell him so, but Ray was in no mood to listen. It took him a while to get over the incident.

But there was another side to Oscar Peterson — a side that came out often in his relationship with his friends and fellow musicians. Oscar loved practical jokes and pranks. Sometimes he would put Herb Ellis's guitar strings out of tune during the intermission of a performance. Then, when they went back out to do the next set, he would distract Herb so that he would forget to tune his guitar before they started to play again.

In 1953, on JATP's first tour in Japan, Oscar tuned the G-string on Ray Brown's bass way down, just as Norman Granz was introducing Ray and Ella Fitzgerald. Ray started to play, only to discover his bass was badly out of tune. Ella Fitzgerald shot Ray some nasty looks as she tried to get through the tune they were playing. Ray Brown took the prank with good humor. He decided to bide his time, waiting for an opportunity to get back at Oscar.

On the break, Ray went out and won a bunch of little steel balls in a Japanese game called pachinko. After intermission, he and some of the other musicians came back out on stage. The lights were still dimmed as Oscar was introduced, and before Oscar had a chance to see what was going on, Ray had spread the steel balls across the piano strings. Oscar sat down at the piano and started to play the introduction to a slow ballad called "But Beautiful," featuring Bill Harris on the trombone. Every note came out "brrr, brrr, brrr," from the vibrations of the balls against the strings.

Oscar caught on at once, and he started taking the balls out of the piano and whipping them across the stage at Ray, hitting Ray's bass as well. Bill Harris was left standing there, watching the balls flying across the stage, abandoned in the middle of his trombone feature.

One time the trio was playing a matinee at the Rouge Lounge in Detroit. When Oscar sat down for the second set, he realized that some of the notes were not working. He turned to Ray and said there was something wrong with the piano. At first Ray played innocent, but then he and Herb started to laugh. Oscar realized his bandmates had him this time. They had taken transparent tape and taped together a few keys here and there, up and down the keyboard.

There are many parts, both good and bad, that make up the life of a touring musician. Oscar, Ray and Herb loved to perform. Night after night they experienced the energy and excitement of playing before a live audience, of communicating with their music and feeling the response of their listeners.

But other parts of their daily lives were less glamorous. They endured long waits at airports and lonely hours in hotel rooms, far away from family and the comforts of home. They often ate meals on the run and rarely got enough sleep. Maybe their pranks and practical jokes helped to relieve the tension and fatigue, even the occasional boredom, they must have felt along the way.

★ ★ ★

By the early 1950s, jazz was facing heavy competition from early rock and roll and rhythm and blues bands. Most jazz musicians had come to accept that their music would never attract the huge audiences that were flocking to hear these other popular styles, but Norman Granz disagreed. He did not believe that jazz had to be difficult music played in small, back-alley clubs with tiny audiences. Granz believed that jazz music should be happy music, melodic and swinging. He wanted audiences to leave his concerts humming the tunes, and to buy his albums so they could keep singing along at home.

By sticking to his vision, Granz enjoyed a degree of success with JATP that probably no other jazz promoter has been able to match. His all-star lineups, featuring some of the great jazz instrumentalists and singers of that time, were a hit with the young, enthusiastic crowds who flocked to his concerts.

Granz decided to take his troupe to Europe, where American jazz had found a large audience. In Europe, black jazz musicians were treated with a dignity and respect they rarely found back home. In 1952, JATP added an annual European tour to its schedule.

The number of concerts JATP performed every year was staggering. In 1954, the troupe played fifty concerts in twenty-five European cities, twenty-four concerts in Japan, and seventy-five concerts throughout the United States and Canada. That same year, Oscar earned five thousand dollars a week as a member of JATP. This was an extremely good salary for anyone at that time, and quite remarkable by jazz standards.

Norman Granz had enough confidence in Oscar's abilities to make him the unofficial musical director of JATP. He was the one who called the tempos of the tunes and kept the concerts running smoothly. From time to time, Oscar was also called upon to settle disputes among the members of the troupe.

Besides touring with JATP and playing with his trio, Oscar was also kept busy in the recording studio. After all, Norman Granz was one of the big jazz record producers of that time. He saw an opportunity to give his musicians greater exposure by recording them frequently. Oscar already had sixteen albums to his credit by the time he was twenty-nine years old.

Oscar, Herb and Ray made many recordings together, some of which have become classics. On August 8, 1956, Granz recorded the trio live at the Stratford Shakespearean Festival in Stratford, Ontario. The album was released on Granz's new label, Verve, and it was both a critical and commercial success. The recording captures the trio's remarkable energy and its bluesy, driving swing. The trio had the "lock-down" working that day.

A few years earlier, Granz had the idea to do a series of albums featuring the music of specific composers such as Duke Ellington and Cole Porter. Oscar and his trio played on several of these albums, accompanying Louis Armstrong, Ella Fitzgerald and other top vocalists. Granz also arranged studio sessions for Oscar with many of the star soloists of JATP.

The fans kept buying the albums, but the critics were less impressed. Many of them believed that even though Oscar was a brilliant player, he was recording too much. They also said that Granz's musicians were worn out from the physical demands of so much touring and recording, so that they were not able to perform at their best.

Granz had never shown much knowledge or even interest in making records with good sound quality. As a result, his recordings had a reputation for being poorly recorded and mixed. The balance was often uneven, with the bass or drums too loud on some. On several the piano was not even in tune. Some critics accused Granz of being more interested in making money than in producing high-quality records.

Oscar Peterson was one of Norman Granz's favorite pianists and closest friends. He and Granz happened to share many of the same ideas about jazz, and Oscar never complained that his manager was recording him too often or making him play too many concerts. Oscar's physical stamina was impressive. He just seemed to accept that as a jazz musician, he would work all the time.

The critics may not have loved everything Oscar was doing, but his fans adored him. *Down Beat*, the best-known jazz magazine in the United States, had an annual poll in which their readers selected their favorite musicians. Oscar Peterson won the *Down Beat* reader's poll as best pianist for six straight years in that period, from 1950 through 1955. By the mid-fifties, the Oscar Peterson Trio was considered one of the top jazz trios in the world

But for all the success the trio was enjoying, the constant pressure of life on the road was taking its toll on one of its members. Herb Ellis was a binge drinker. He didn't drink all the time, but sometimes, when the band had a few days off, he would start to drink heavily, and then he would be very sick. Because Herb never drank on the job, it took a long time for his friends to realize there was something wrong.

One time JATP was about to embark on a tour of Europe. Everyone in the troupe met in New York for the flight overseas, but Herb Ellis never showed up. Oscar and Ray had to leave for Europe without him, beside themselves with worry. By this time the three of them had developed a closeness that went way beyond an ordinary working relationship. For years they had been all but inseparable, and they loved one another like brothers.

Norman Granz was equally concerned. For although he could be a difficult and prickly person, time and again he had shown that he could be a compassionate and caring man, especially with his musicians. He hired a detective agency to find Herb, and someone finally managed to track him down. He had been hospitalized in New York after turning himself in to Alcoholics Anonymous, an organization that runs a program to help alcoholics stop drinking.

Oscar Peterson was very naive about alcohol addiction, and at first he didn't understand the seriousness of Herb Ellis's problem. When Herb rejoined the group in Hamburg, Germany, a city known for its beer gardens, Oscar suggested that they go out for a beer together. His motives were totally sincere. He was happy to have his buddy back, and he couldn't imagine there was anything wrong in having a couple of beers. They went out for a few drinks, and Herb seemed okay, and he completed the tour with the band.

A year later Herb disappeared again, this time for a month. In the meantime, Oscar had taken the time to become more educated about alcohol addiction. When Herb surfaced again in New York, Oscar talked to him on the phone and told him to fly out and join the band in Los Angeles.

Herb said that he didn't think that Oscar would want him back. Oscar said, "I don't want to go through all this. Get on a plane and get out here." When Herb arrived, Oscar had a long talk with him, and this time he didn't mince his words. He didn't scold him. He just made him understand that Herb's drinking was hurting himself and his friends. Oscar said that at some point, Herb "finally bought it." Herb Ellis went back to Alcoholics Anonymous, and this time he quit drinking for good.

Still, it was clear that he needed a break from the frantic pace of almost constant touring and recording. In 1958, Herb decided to leave the trio, taking a job as accompanist to Ella Fitzgerald and settling in California with his family. It was hard for Oscar and Ray when Herb left the band, but they realized it was the right thing to do. Herb Ellis became one of the busiest studio musicians in Los Angeles. This gave him the opportunity to keep playing music without having to travel so much.

★ ★ ★

By the early fifties, Oscar Peterson had met and played with many of the great jazz musicians of the period, but when he finally met his idol, Art Tatum, it was a special occasion. To Oscar, Art Tatum was the best — "The greatest living instrumentalist of them all," as he once told *Time* magazine.

Oscar was not a timid man, but there was something about Tatum that left him almost frozen with awe. "I was totally frightened of this man and his tremendous talent," Oscar said. "It's like a lion: you're scared to death, but it's such a beautiful animal, you want to come up close and hear it roar."

Soon after he had started his trio with Ray and Herb, Oscar was playing at Louis and Alex's, a club in Washington, D.C. One night Art Tatum came in to listen. Ray Brown knew how Oscar felt about Tatum, and he whispered to him that he saw Tatum sitting over at the bar. All the feelings Oscar had built up over the years about his hero came rushing to the surface, and it was an effort for him just to finish the set.

After the gig, Oscar and Ray went with Tatum to an after-hours club, where Tatum asked Oscar to play. Oscar was too scared, so he refused. Tatum was almost totally blind, but maybe he heard the fear in Oscar's voice, and he told Oscar this story. He said that there was an old man in Kansas City who only knew one chorus of the blues. Yet every time Tatum went to Kansas City, he went to hear the old man play. "Nobody plays the blues like him," Tatum explained. "Everyone has something to say in music — if he has some talent and has the discipline to master even one chorus."

Tatum's words calmed Oscar enough to allow him to play something for his idol, but his playing was tentative, without his usual assurance and poise. Then Tatum played for Oscar, and Oscar said, "It fractured me."

Oscar and Art Tatum became good friends, but it took

Oscar a long time to get over his fear about playing in front of Tatum. Finally Tatum told him, "You can't afford this. You have too much going for you. If you have to hate me when I walk into the room, I don't care. I want you to play." Gradually Oscar began to relax more, until one day he realized he wasn't scared anymore.

In November 1956, Oscar was playing in San Francisco when he got a phone call from the trumpet player, Harry (Sweets) Edison, telling him that Art Tatum was dying. Edison told Oscar to come to Los Angeles as soon as he could to say his good-byes. Oscar couldn't get out of his club date that night, but as soon as he finished work, he flew down to Los Angeles. When he got there, Edison called him at his hotel to tell him that he was too late. Art Tatum was dead.

Oscar was planning to stay for the funeral when he got another call, this one from his sister in Montreal. Their father, Daniel Peterson, had just died of a stroke. With a heavy heart, Oscar immediately returned home. "In one week," he said, "I lost two of the best friends I had."

★ ★ ★

There is a long tradition in the arts of passing knowledge to the next generation. The master passes on the torch to the successor, who then carries on, filled with the spirit of the past and new hope for the future. Art Tatum once said to Oscar, "I know I can play the piano, and you know you can play the piano. I wanna make one thing clear to you. This is my time. When I'm finished — you got it." At that moment, Oscar knew that Tatum had chosen him, out of all the piano players around, to carry the torch next. Nothing could have meant more to him than those few words from his idol.

After Tatum died, Oscar visited Tatum's wife at their home. It was a painful visit for Oscar, whose eyes kept traveling to the Steinway grand piano in the corner of the living room. It was all covered up now, forever silent.

"I still think about that," Oscar once said. "Every time I play."

Herb Ellis (1921–)

Mitchell Herbert Ellis grew up in a small town in Texas, where he learned to play the harmonica and banjo before settling on the guitar. Later he studied music at North Texas State University. There his friends urged him to listen to the brilliant jazz guitarist, Charlie Christian, one of the black musicians Benny Goodman hired for his band.

Ellis had never heard the guitar played that way before, and it took him a while to catch on to what Christian was doing. When he did, he said that it hit him like a spiritual awakening. Almost overnight, he became determined to learn that same swinging, bluesy guitar style. For a while he played in a territory band, and later he landed a job with Jimmy Dorsey, one of the most popular swing-band leaders of the period. Then he played with the trio Soft Winds, until Oscar Peterson offered him a spot in his trio.

In his years with Oscar, Herb Ellis became known for his technical virtuosity, his ability to play with dazzling speed and quiet lyricism. He became equally accomplished in his roles as a soloist in the trio and as an accompanist to Oscar and Ray. After he left the trio in 1958, he spent several years as Ella Fitzgerald's accompanist before settling in Los Angeles as a studio musician.

In 1973 Herb became part of a group called Great Guitars, joining Joe Pass and Barney Kessel — both of them also worked with Oscar Peterson — and a fourth guitarist, Charlie Byrd. He performed and recorded regularly with this group and many others through the 1980s and 1990s.

In the early 1990s, at the time of his reunion with Oscar and Ray, Herb recalled touring with JATP through the segregated South, and his feelings when the white musicians stayed at a hotel for whites, while the black musicians left to go to the hotel that would serve them. Herb Ellis always stayed at the black hotel, preferring to remain with his friends, Oscar and Ray. As he said, in his simple and direct way, "I couldn't find any reason not to." At the JVC Jazz Festival in 1998, Herb Ellis was honored with an evening of performances devoted to his career.

9

The Teacher

By the late 1950s, the club scene in Montreal had changed. Dancers had replaced musicians in many clubs, and Oscar was finding fewer good playing opportunities. He was working quite often in Toronto, anyway, so it made sense to make that city his home base.

In the summer of 1958, he and his family moved from Montreal to Scarborough, a suburb of Toronto. Oscar and Lil now had five young children. After Lynn and Sharon, Gay, Oscar Jr. and Norman were born one year apart. When the Petersons bought their new house, they found out that their white neighbors were thinking about starting a petition to prevent them from moving in. Oscar decided to go ahead with the move anyway. He knew that the law was on his side, and he figured that his neighbors would just have to get used to the new family on the street.

The Petersons stayed, and gradually some of their neighbors came around to the idea of having a famous pianist in their midst, even if he was black. Eventually his name even drew people to the area. Oscar's friends would tease him, asking if he was getting a commission for all the houses he was helping to sell.

After years of total dedication to his music, Oscar was enjoying a level of financial comfort that he could not have imagined as a child growing up in St. Antoine. Now he had the money, and at least some free time, to explore areas of life other than music.

He developed a passion for photography, and he would buy expensive equipment for his new hobby, only to replace it when a newer, better system came along. He even bought a miniature darkroom to take on the road with him. Many nights he would return to his hotel room and spend hours developing and printing negatives of pictures he had taken. As his interest developed, he enrolled in some correspondence courses, which Lil would mail to him when he was away from home. He tried to keep his interest under control, though. He knew that every hour he spent with his photography was time away from his music.

And now, with Herb Ellis gone from the band, Oscar had the difficult job of finding another musician to take his spot. In their six years together, Oscar, Ray and Herb had created something special. Oscar was too wise to imagine that anyone could simply step in and fill Herb's shoes. Instead, he decided to go for a completely different sound, to replace the guitar with drums.

First he hired drummer Gene Gammage, who stayed with the trio for only a short while in 1958. Then Oscar decided to try out another drummer, Ed Thigpen. As soon as they started to play, Oscar knew that he had the makings of another great band.

Ed was the son of the accomplished jazz drummer, Ben Thigpen. His parents separated when he was young, and he moved to Los Angeles with his mother. Despite this, his father's influence remained strong, and Ed began to play the drums when he was still quite young. When he was twenty-one, he got a job with the Cootie Williams band, playing at the Savoy Ballroom in New York.

In 1952, he began his military service. When he was discharged from the army, he went to Japan for what the army calls R and R — rest and relaxation. As it happened, JATP was on tour in Japan at the same time. Ed met Oscar on that trip, and when he heard the trio play, he was blown away by their sound, and by their ability to "swing so hard." Ed pulled Ray aside and told him that the only thing the band was missing was a drummer. Ray just shrugged and said, "Well, y'never know, kid."

After his discharge, Ed Thigpen returned to New York and the jazz scene there, playing with some of the finest musicians of his generation. But he never forgot the experience of hearing the Oscar Peterson Trio, and his dream that one day he would have a chance to play with them.

In 1958, when Oscar actually offered him the job, Ed could hardly believe his good fortune. He was almost star-struck, in awe of his bandmates. He also felt a lot of pressure to live up to their expectations. By joining the band, Ed had become a member of the highest-paid and most recognized jazz trio in the world.

Backed by just drums and bass, Oscar now had greater freedom in his choice of voicings than he had when Herb was in the band. But Ed Thigpen's presence led to other important changes as well. A skilled jazz drummer uses tone and rhythm to create a huge palette of sound, and Oscar was eager to explore this with his new trio. Ed was a master with brushes, which a drummer often uses on ballads or quiet tunes. On some tunes the trio would start with Ed on brushes, with Ray playing "two" choruses, half notes on beats one and three of the bar. At some point in the tune Ed would switch to the sticks and ride cymbal with Ray playing quarter notes behind him, and the band would go into what Oscar called the "steaming zone." As the volume increased, so did the band's intensity.

Jazz musicians use devices like these to express a wide range of sounds and moods. One goal of most bands, large or small, is to create a sound that is distinctly theirs. Oscar was able to achieve this with his trios. Most knowledgeable jazz fans could hear a recording of Oscar, Ray and Ed — or of Oscar, Ray and Herb before that — and recognize it as the Oscar Peterson Trio.

Ed Thigpen was not given much time to find his way in the trio. Soon after he joined the band, Norman Granz booked them for a four-week run at the London House in Chicago. As if that weren't enough, Granz also decided to send them into the studio during the day to re-record most of the tunes that Oscar and Ray had previously recorded. In six days the trio cut 124 tracks, an astonishing number in such a brief time.

Most of the tracks were very short, with little time set aside for improvising. This was very different from what happened in the trio's club or concert performances, when solos might last for many minutes, as Oscar, Ray and Ed took turns improvising on chorus after chorus of the tune. Some of the music critics complained that these latest recordings were throwaways, not up to the trio's usual standards.

Maybe so, but by the end of this intense period of performing and recording, Ed Thigpen was fitting into the trio like a hand in a well-worn glove. Oscar says that the band was so locked-in, that often he did not even have to call the next tune. He would just say, "Okay, it's here. One, two," and Ed and Ray would know instinctively what Oscar was about to play.

Ed Thigpen spent the next six years as a member of the Oscar Peterson Trio. Oscar has called that period "six years of unbelievable music."

★ ★ ★

The fifties were coming to an end, and Oscar could look back on an incredible decade of performing and recording. His work with his trios had probably earned him the most attention, but he was also seen as one of the most important accompanists of the period.

It was his manager, Norman Granz, who saw how suited he was for this role. Granz set up recording sessions with Oscar — and often the entire trio — accompanying many of the great jazz soloists of the day. Out of these sessions came albums with saxophone giants Lester Young, Coleman Hawkins and Charlie Parker; trumpeters Louis Armstrong and Dizzy Gillespie; and vocalists Billie Holiday and Ella Fitzgerald, among others.

When he was accompanying other players, Oscar showed a remarkable ability to control his strong, even overpowering presence and let the soloists shine. He knew that different players looked for different things from an accompanist, and he tried to adjust his playing to suit the situation. He once said, "The interesting thing is that people see you playing for different soloists and they take it for granted that, well, if you can play for one, you can play for them all. But as you can realise, they all approach their solo thing differently."

He said that Stan Getz, the tenor saxophone player, liked a lush, percussive cushion underneath him. Another tenor player, Ben Webster, liked more of a harmonic flow. Dizzy

Gillespie, on the other hand, wanted a hot, fiery accompaniment. Oscar said that it was a challenge to accompany these great artists.

And many of the musicians loved to work with Oscar. Ben Webster said that Oscar was the best accompanying pianist he ever had. He said that Oscar listened to the horn players — saxophone, trumpet, trombone, etc. — and seemed to know exactly what they were going to play. Then he would set up the perfect accompaniment for them — one that both supported what they were doing and pushed them to reach for more.

Ella Fitzgerald would listen to Oscar and be inspired by his beautiful touch on the piano. She said that his sound "makes you want to sing, it makes you want to do what you're doing." That was quite a compliment, coming as it did from one of the great jazz vocalists of all time.

In the fifties, Oscar and his trios were Norman Granz's workhorses, prepared to take on all the jobs that Granz sent their way. They developed a reputation for working harder and recording more than perhaps any other group in the history of jazz. They kept going, night after night and year after year, with almost no time off.

But by 1960, even the workhorses were ready for a break, or at least a change in the routine. For some time, Oscar and Ray had been talking about setting up some kind of a jazz school. After all, other musicians were always coming up to them, asking questions about the music, seeking direction and advice from the masters.

In the early days of jazz, there was no such thing as a school where young musicians could study. Jazz had always been a music that was passed on from one player to the next. It was a music that came, at least in part, from the blues, played by musicians who did not always even read music. But by the time Oscar and Ray were thinking of starting their own school, jazz had gained much wider acceptance as a musical form worthy of serious study.

By then there were thousands of stage-band programs in high schools, colleges and universities throughout the United States. There were also several well-known schools that offered degrees in jazz studies and performance. These included the Berklee School of Music in Boston, the Juilliard School of Music in New York, and Herb Ellis's old school, North Texas State University.

Many of these schools had jazz ensembles, where students were given some practical experience playing in small or large groups. Professional jazz musicians would lead the ensembles, but for the most part, the students had only limited opportunity to play with their teachers.

Oscar and Ray were aware of these other schools, and they wanted to offer something a little different. They believed that young musicians would learn more quickly if they were given the chance to play regularly with experienced jazz musicians, instead of playing only with other musicians at their level.

They talked to Ed Thigpen about their idea, and he quickly jumped on board. Then they approached two other musicians — trombonist Butch Watanabe and clarinetist and composer Phil Nimmons. Both Watanabe and Nimmons were accomplished Canadian jazz musicians, and they were eager to be part of a new jazz school in Canada.

In January 1960, Oscar and his friends opened the Advanced School of Contemporary Music — ASCM, for short — in downtown Toronto. They proceeded cautiously, since none of them had any experience running a school of this sort. In a way, the first few months of ASCM were an experiment, a chance for the teachers and students to work on a new approach to teaching and studying jazz.

Within a year, ASCM was in a sixteen-room house, and the teachers had as many students as they could manage. They had hit upon a formula, and the formula seemed to be working. The students had one-on-one instruction, and then they had the chance to play in a trio or a larger group that often included the teachers themselves. A piano student would take a lesson with Oscar Peterson and then have the opportunity to play with Ray Brown and Ed Thigpen, and so on.

Then there were master classes — the teachers called them forums — in which the students had to perform before the other students and teachers. Afterwards, the teachers would discuss the performance and offer suggestions. Oscar might have told a student in her lesson that she had played a bad chord, but it might not mean much to her until she tried to play it with Ray Brown backing her on bass. Then, as Oscar remembered, Ray might stop the student and say, "What was that chord? I can't find any note to play."

To play jazz almost always means learning to work with other people. It involves listening and then responding to music that is being made up by another musician right on the spot. It takes a special training to learn how to do that, and countless hours of practical on-the-job experience, practicing and playing with other musicians. The Advanced School of Contemporary Music was giving students this training, using a different approach from any other jazz school at the time.

But Oscar expected his students to do more than just learn to play their instruments. He believed that they should also have a thorough knowledge of the major figures in jazz history. He assigned records for them to listen to, and some of his students complained about this. They had been listening to jazz for years, they said, and didn't need to be told what they should listen to.

Oscar would challenge them on how much they really knew. "Describe the background supplied behind the trumpet solo," he would say. "Didn't hear that? Can you tell whether the drummer played sticks or brushes in this part of the record? Harmonic structure? Form of the tune?" Soon he had the students listening in a new way, and with greater respect, to the musicians of the past.

ASCM was a school for serious and talented young jazz musicians, several of whom — including Wray Downes, Carol Britto and Doug Riley — went on to have successful careers in jazz.

★ ★ ★

Even while they were busy running their school, Oscar and the other musicians still had their own careers to take care of. For Oscar and the trio, that meant dealing with a number of big changes. By the early sixties, Norman Granz had grown tired of the record business. As his company, Verve, got bigger and bigger, he had become less interested in some of the albums it was producing.

He was also watching the new generation of jazz musicians coming up, bringing with them different ways of playing. Avant-garde jazz, sometimes called "free" jazz, had broken away from traditional harmony and was exploring new approaches to improvisation. Granz had little sympathy for these new approaches. In 1961, he sold Verve to MGM Records for almost three million dollars. He retired from the record business, although he continued to manage the careers of Oscar and a few other of his favorite artists.

Jim Davis, Oscar's new record producer, had very different ideas about how to record Oscar. He had little interest in churning out more of those "theme" albums — albums featuring the music of an individual composer or Broadway musical — that Oscar had made under Norman Granz. Why not record Oscar the way he really sounded, when he and his trio were playing in the clubs?

In 1962, under Davis's direction, Oscar, Ray and Ed made four albums at the London House in Chicago. This time the critics had nicer things to say, rating these albums among the best the trio had made together. In that same year, the trio made a studio album called *Night Train*, which soon became one of Oscar's biggest-selling albums.

Oscar and the trio continued to record and perform, but they were not able to keep the same schedule they had before they opened their school. Soon they began to miss the intensity and excitement that came from playing all the time. Oscar had a fully equipped music studio in his basement. When he was feeling restless, he would invite Ray and Ed over, and the three of them would play for hours. Oscar said that some of the best playing he ever did was in the basement with his trio.

Sometimes, because of his responsibility to his school, Oscar would have to turn down a concert or club engagement. This was a hard decision for him. Not only had he spent most of his life playing at every possible opportunity, but he had also grown accustomed to a standard of living for himself and his family that now seemed threatened.

The Petersons lived in a nice house in the suburbs, and Oscar had been able to buy new cars for himself and Lil. It was important for him to see that his children were well dressed, that they had their music lessons and toys and books. His music studio and photography were also extremely expensive. If he wanted to continue to live in this way, he knew he could not really afford a big cut to his income.

And there were other problems as well. Many of the students were young, struggling jazz musicians when they started at ASCM, and they were having trouble supporting themselves over the five months of the school year. For a while ASCM went to a one-month term, to try to ease the money problem for both teachers and students. Even this seemed only a temporary solution. In 1964, Oscar and the other teachers decided to close the Advanced School of Contemporary Music.

In that same year, Oscar's twenty-year marriage to Lil was also coming to an end. His constant traveling and his focus on his work had placed a great strain on their marriage. Lil had been a shy teenager when she and Oscar first met, and she was swept off her feet by the brilliant young pianist with charm to spare. But soon there were young children to look after, and the responsibility for their care fell mainly on Lil's shoulders. Oscar always took good care of his family's financial needs, but in many other ways, it was as if Lil was a single mother, raising five children by herself. Then Oscar would come home again, usually for a couple of weeks at a time. All of a sudden Lil's life would be very different.

Oscar would want to invite his musician friends over for dinner, or he would take Lil down to the club to hear the band play. Suddenly there were all these famous musicians hanging around, and the shy and retiring Lil found this very difficult to handle.

Oscar saw that he and Lil were growing farther apart. While he was traveling all over the world, meeting new people and being exposed to new things, Lil was living a quiet, secluded life with their young children. When it became clear that they would not be able to work out their differences, Oscar and Lil separated and later divorced.

By then Oscar had already met Sandra King at a club in Toronto. She was a nurse at the Toronto General Hospital and a great jazz fan. Before long Sandra and Oscar were together constantly; she even stopped working so that she could travel with him when he went on the road.

Oscar and Sandra decided to get married, but from the very beginning, their relationship was full of turmoil. Sandra was white, and Oscar later admitted that their different racial backgrounds brought a certain tension to the marriage. A bigger problem was that Oscar and Sandra were both strong-willed people determined to get their way, except that their ways often ran in opposite directions. Oscar and Sandra were together for fifteen years, but their marriage would also end in divorce.

★ ★ ★

Within a very short period, Oscar had closed his school, divorced and remarried. Then in 1965, Ed Thigpen decided to leave the trio. Eventually he settled in Denmark, where he became an important player on the European jazz scene.

Ray Brown's turn was next. He and Oscar had spent fifteen years together, mostly on the road, traveling from one job to another. He was worn out, plain and simple. In a 1967 interview in *Down Beat* magazine, Brown recalled that the band had had a stretch of forty-seven one-nighters in 1965 without one day off. "Frankly, at that pace," Ray said, "I don't need that kind of money, because it only can be used in the hospital sooner or later." He followed Herb Ellis's path and settled in California. There he had as much work as he wanted, without having to travel all the time.

Oscar had now lost two beloved sidemen, but leaving his life on the road was not an option. His need to perform and his love of the limelight were just too powerful to resist. As he once said, "I could never think of giving up what I'm doing. I could never, for instance, settle down and become a studio musician. That kind of job was offered to me years ago, but it doesn't represent the way I want to live."

Before very long Ray and Herb would arrive at the same conclusion themselves and return to touring. And although they did not know it then, one day the trio would be reunited. For the time being, though, one of the closest associations in jazz had come to an end.

Ella Fitzgerald (1917–1996)

Ella Jane Fitzgerald became one of the most successful and respected jazz vocalists of all time, but her childhood was filled with trouble and despair. When she was about four years old, her father abandoned her, and later she was abused by her stepfather. From a very young age, Ella found comfort and joy in singing and dancing, and she sang regularly at her church in Yonkers, New York.

In 1932, when Ella was fourteen, she got a job as a dancer. Then her mother died, and Ella moved to Harlem to live with her aunt. When she dropped out of high school, she was sent to a juvenile home for truancy, but before long she ran away from the home. For almost two years she lived on the streets of Harlem. She survived by working for gamblers, acting as a lookout for a neighbor-hood brothel, and by dancing and singing for tips.

In November 1934, Ella entered an amateur contest at the famed Apollo Theatre. She had intended to dance in the contest, but when she compared her second-hand clothes and men's boots with the clothing of the other dancers, she decided to sing instead. The Apollo audiences were harsh judges, and Ella was nervous as she stepped into the spotlight. Then she began to sing, and she brought down the house. Her first-prize victory was supposed to bring her a week's work at the Apollo, but the manager refused to hire her, saying that she wasn't pretty enough.

She returned to the streets but continued to enter other contests. Word of the talented singer began to spread, and in April 1935, she got an offer to sing with the great Chick Webb Orchestra, which performed at the Savoy Ballroom in Harlem.

Although Ella had no formal training, her excellent intonation, huge vocal range and infectious swing made her a hit with other musicians and with the public. After her debut with Chick Webb, she performed and recorded with the leading bands of the period. With her hit recordings of "A-tisket, A-tasket" and "Undecided," she went from being a well-known jazz singer to a star. When Chick Webb died in 1939, Ella took over the orchestra, which was renamed Ella Fitzgerald and Her Famous Orchestra. She remained with it until 1942, when she decided to pursue a solo career.

For several years she was married to Ray Brown and performed with his trio. In 1949 she joined Norman Granz's Jazz at the Philharmonic, and over her long career as a member of Granz's troupe, she gained worldwide fame. She worked frequently with Oscar Peterson, Duke Ellington and Count Basie.

Ella Fitzgerald sang with a virtuosity equal to that of the best jazz instrumentalists. Her scat singing (made-up syllables without words) became one of her trademarks, and she could improvise melodic lines in the style of the great jazz horn players. She influenced generations of American singers, both jazz and popular, and left a legacy of recordings and performances that rank among the best in jazz.

10

Going Solo

In the 1960s, Oscar Peterson became friends with a wealthy German businessman, Hans Georg Brunner-Schwer. The two had much in common, including their size, their love of jazz and their fascination with sound and technology. Like Oscar, Brunner-Schwer had perfect pitch, but he did not become a musician. Instead, he became a master sound engineer. On his estate in Villingen, a small city near the Swiss border, Brunner-Schwer built a wonderful recording studio where he would invite his favorite jazz musicians to play for him and a small group of invited guests.

Oscar Peterson went to Villingen with Ray Brown and Ed Thigpen in the fall of 1963. That first visit was so successful that for the next nine years Oscar made annual trips to Villingen to perform and record.

For the musicians, this was a gig made in heaven. Brunner-Schwer and his wife fed them delicious meals, making them feel at home on their large, beautiful estate. Each morning they woke up to the inviting aroma of freshly ground coffee, a luxury they had rarely experienced in their years on the road.

While they were recording, they could look out at the spectacular grounds and watch the gardeners at work.

Never before had Oscar and his bandmates played in such a warm, comfortable atmosphere. In the audience there might be twenty or so guests, fans of American jazz who were delighted to be part of such a cozy gathering. Sometimes, though, Oscar would sit down at the piano by himself. And the piano that Brunner-Schwer provided for him was a treasure: a nine-foot German Steinway, considered one of the finest concert pianos in the world.

Before Oscar started to play, Brunner-Schwer would set up his microphones, which he placed much closer to the strings of the piano than was commonly done at that time. Then he would go upstairs to his studio to record the performance. He even set up a closed-circuit television in the studio, so he was able to see Oscar and the other musicians while they played.

For the first time in his career, Oscar was being recorded in a way that showed off the true brilliance of his sound. He would have liked nothing more than to have the tapes released to the public, but at the time this was not possible. During the first few years he went to Villingen, he was under contract to another record company, Limelight. Under the terms of that contract, Oscar was not allowed to make recordings for commercial sale with any other company.

He and Brunner-Schwer would sit and listen to the tapes, and Oscar would shake his head, resigned to having some of his best recordings remain in his friend's private collection. Finally, in 1968, Oscar's contract with Limelight expired, and he and Brunner-Schwer were free to release some of the Villingen performances.

By that time, Brunner-Schwer had his own record label, MPS, short for Musik Produktion Schwarzwald. He and

Oscar sifted through the hours of tapes they had made over the years and selected enough music to release four albums on the MPS label. One was called *The Way I Really Play*, a title that let people know exactly how Oscar felt about these recordings.

In all, Oscar made fifteen albums for MPS, and both fans and critics said they were among the best of his career. Of the fifteen, two were solo albums: *My Favorite Instrument* and *Tracks*. This was a new direction for Oscar, who had only recently started to think about playing more solo piano. He once said that *My Favorite Instrument* was his best album ever. "Perhaps it was because it was the first album where I was completely free," he explained, "and in which I did what I felt like."

★ ★ ★

The piano is the most orchestral of all the instruments. It can supply the bass, the harmony and even the percussion for a piece of music all by itself. But a pianist in a group has to take into account the range and capabilities of the other instruments in deciding what to play or not to play. When Oscar was playing with his trios, he knew that the bassist would take most of the responsibility for the bottom end of the band's sound. The guitar added both harmony and percussion — guitarists often strum quarter-note rhythms when they are "comping" or accompanying other soloists — and the drummer provided a strong rhythmic and percussive lift.

When Oscar began to think about playing more solo piano, he realized that he would have to take over the roles of these other musicians. Because he had always been a very strong two-handed player, the challenge was more mental than physical. He knew that it was one thing for him to play two-handed piano with a rhythm section — bass and guitar or drums —

backing him up, and quite another to be out there on his own. Many pianists throw in a bit of solo playing even when they are in a group, but this is a far cry from playing a whole album by yourself.

At that time Oscar was still leading a trio, one of several he had put together after Ray Brown and Ed Thigpen left the band. This left him facing a big decision. He could stick with his trio and do the kind of work he had been doing for the past twenty years, or he could set off in a new direction.

He found himself turning to the people he most trusted for advice about his career. Both Duke Ellington and Norman Granz had been urging him for quite some time to try solo piano in his club and concert engagements. Duke Ellington insisted that Oscar's fans wanted the chance to hear him by himself, without a rhythm section.

Oscar thought things over and decided to go solo. He broke up his trio and, in 1972, he played his first solo concert at Carnegie Hall, where he had made his spectacular U.S. debut twenty-three years earlier. The concert was part of the Newport Jazz Festival, and it was a great success. He followed it up with a long solo engagement at the El Matador Club in San Francisco.

After so many years of playing with other musicians, Oscar was thrilled with the freedom that came with being a solo performer. When he was part of a group, he saw it as his responsibility to set up what was coming next, to give his bandmates time to react. Now, if he wanted to go off in another direction, there was no reason for him not to. "In a group," he said, "you play with a sense of a pact that you're going to do a tune in a particular way, within certain confines. If you suddenly decide to take a left turn down a one-way street, it becomes a little hazardous for the group!"

As much fun as he was having with his solo career, Oscar never intended to give up his group playing. Within a year he had formed a new trio, this one with guitarist Joe Pass and bassist Niels-Henning Ørsted Pedersen. His solo playing, however, became an important part of his career. During the next two decades, he would combine solo and group work, in both recordings and performances.

But simply playing music, in a group or as a soloist, was not enough for Oscar. His need to keep learning and to explore new areas remained a big part of his character, as it had ever since he was a small boy. His interest in photography was just one example of that curiosity. He also knew an immense amount about audio equipment and the technology behind it.

Over the many hours he had spent with his friend, Brunner-Schwer, Oscar learned more than most musicians about sound engineering. Later he became interested in synthesizers and electronic music, and he set out to learn everything he could about that area as well.

So it is no surprise that when Oscar began to compose his own music, he went about it in quite a serious way. Most jazz musicians write at least some music. For some of them, composing means putting down on paper (or working out in their heads) short songs or melodies. Sometimes they borrow the chord changes from the blues or other well-known pop songs, and they make up their own melodies to fit the chords.

Then, of course, there are musicians who have become as famous for their compositions as they have for their playing. Duke Ellington was a famous big-band leader, but he is also considered by many to be one of the best American composers of the twentieth century. Ellington wrote hundreds of songs. Some were short pieces that could stand on their own, but he also wrote longer compositions.

From early in his career, Oscar started writing short compositions. He recorded "Oscar's Boogie" in 1947, and through the fifties, he wrote many blues and some ballads. Often he named them after close friends or family. But the music he began to write in the sixties was longer and more serious.

Canadiana Suite was Oscar's first try at writing connected pieces, rather than short, individual tunes. It is made up of eight separate melodies, each one named after a different place in Canada, going from east to west. In 1964 he recorded the entire suite on an album with Ray Brown and Ed Thigpen.

When he wrote *Canadiana Suite*, it was more than twenty years since Oscar had left Canada for life on the road. Since then, except for the short period when he ran his school in Toronto, he had rarely spent more than a few weeks each year at home.

But Oscar never stopped loving the country where he was born, and it is interesting that his first long composition is a tribute to Canada. One of the pieces in the suite, "Place St. Henri," honors the part of Montreal where he was born. It is a bouncy, up-tempo tune that reveals the many happy memories Oscar had of those early days.

Even though Oscar first recorded *Canadiana Suite* with his trio, he felt that the compositions would work better as piano pieces. In later years, he recorded individual pieces from the suite for solo piano.

Oscar also wrote music that expressed his feelings about being a black man during a time of great struggle for equal rights. He was very affected by his own experiences with racism and discrimination, and he was moved by the uplifting words of the great leaders of the civil rights movement. "Hymn to Freedom," which Oscar wrote in 1962 for his *Night Train* album, was his way of showing his feelings about the struggle. The piece has elements of gospel and blues music all rolled up together. It is both happy and sad, hopeful and despairing, an expression of the powerful emotions of that time.

In its original form, "Hymn to Freedom" was an instrumental piece played by Oscar with Ray Brown and Ed Thigpen. After *Night Train* was released, Norman Granz hired Harriette Hamilton to write lyrics for the piece, and "Hymn to Freedom" became a well-known song within the civil rights movement. Since that time it has been performed by youth choirs around the world.

★ ★ ★

Oscar began to experiment with synthesizers when he was composing. He became interested in them partly because of his endless curiosity about technology and gadgets, and partly because they were a useful tool. He had always liked to write music, but he was an impatient composer. Ideas would come to him as he sat at the piano, but the process of writing them down, especially many parts for many instruments, could be long and boring.

And even after he had written the parts, there was more waiting. Before he began to use synthesizers, he would have to hire musicians to learn the parts, so he could hear how well they worked together. Synthesizers did away with all this waiting.

A synthesizer is an electronic instrument that can make a wide range of sounds. Synthesizers come in many shapes and sizes, but electronic keyboards are probably the most common. Oscar could press buttons or move switches on his synthesizer keyboard to make it sound like any instrument or combination of instruments he wanted — from a single string or brass instrument, woodwinds or drums, to an entire orchestra or big band. Then he could combine the different parts, and right away he would know if they worked together or not.

Oscar's approach to learning about synthesizers was very methodical. He went to experts in the field and asked them to teach him everything they knew. The people he talked to were very helpful, and before long he was buying more equipment for his basement studio.

★ ★ ★

As his fourth decade in music came to an end, Oscar's career seemed to have settled into a steady routine. He continued to travel around the globe, performing in concert halls and clubs, and at major jazz festivals. In the early seventies, Norman Granz returned as a record producer with Pablo Records, and he began recording Oscar again, both on solo piano and with his different groups.

History of an Artist is a two-volume collection recorded in 1972 and 1973 that takes the listener through Oscar's career, from his early days up to the time of the recordings. For this album, Norman Granz brought in some of the musicians Oscar had played with over the years and recorded them in different ensemble combinations. For instance, there are duo tracks with Ray Brown, as well as trio and solo performances.

But while Oscar's career might have seemed almost calm and predictable, his personal life continued to be stormy. His marriage to Sandra King ended in 1976. Not long after his divorce, Oscar was on tour in Europe when he met Charlotte Huber, a young Swiss flight attendant. They were married, and in 1978, their son, Joel, was born.

Although Oscar has always been very open about his public life, he has fought hard to keep his private life away from the public eye. Little seems to be known about what happened in his marriage to Charlotte, but soon they were divorced. For a time Charlotte continued to live in Toronto so that Oscar was able to have regular visits with his young son. Then she and Joel moved to eastern Canada, and Oscar lost contact with his son. He once called this "a dreadful loss."

By this time Oscar was in his mid-fifties, and the years of constant travel and work were beginning to catch up with him. He had always been a very big man, but at times his weight soared. This happened when he tried to quit smoking, which he did more than once.

There was a history of arthritis in Oscar's family. He first noticed stiffness in his hands when he was still a teenager, but he almost never complained about it, and did everything he could to keep going, despite his discomfort. His fellow musicians knew, though, that on some nights, he was playing in a lot of pain. By the early 1980s, he was finding the pain more difficult to ignore, and sometimes he had to cancel dates.

During the times when his arthritis was especially bothersome, he would simply turn more to his composing and arranging. He felt very lucky to be a musician. He knew there was always something he could do, even as he got older. "That's the beautiful thing about this profession," he once said, "you can continue learning. The challenge is always there."

★ ★ ★

One day Oscar and his son, Oscar Jr., were raking leaves in front of their cottage in Haliburton, Ontario, when a man drove by and stopped his car. He told them that he needed a gardener. "Would you come over and do my place next?" he asked. Oscar didn't bat an eye. "Yeah," he told the man, "as soon as we finish my place." The man expressed surprise and quickly drove away, his face red with embarrassment.

Many years had passed since Oscar had experienced discrimination in his hometown of Montreal and on his travels through the South. Yet here was one more incident that told him things had not improved nearly as quickly as they should. Oscar was tired of struggling against racism, tired of seeing things around him that he knew were wrong and unfair. He had never been particularly involved in political or social issues, but now, as his career began to slow down, he had a little more time to think about things, and to see injustices that he felt he must stand up to.

One night in the early eighties, Oscar was watching television at home. He began to notice that there were almost no blacks, or any other visible minorities, in the commercials. This ignited a deep anger in him. He had convinced himself that Canadians were much more tolerant about racial issues than Americans, but these commercials told a different story.

From all the time he had spent in the United States, he knew that in this area, the Americans were way ahead. In the States, he had been seeing blacks and other minorities in television commercials and in magazine advertisements for many years.

At the time, the writer Gene Lees was interviewing him for *Toronto Life* magazine, and Oscar spoke freely about this issue, expressing his anger at Canadians who criticized Americans for being racists but ignored what was going on in their own country: "We're all human beings, and we've got the same kind of bigotry and greed as the rest of the world. We can't point the finger any more."

Long after the interview was printed, Oscar continued to speak out about this issue. He said that what really got him about the commercials was that all of them showed the good life in Canada — people having a party or fishing or playing sports — and yet not a single commercial showed anyone who was not white. "It was a blatant affront to all the races that make up the fabric of Canada," he said.

Oscar's comments began to attract some attention. He had never spoken out in this way before — he had much preferred to let his music do the talking. But when a well-known person decides to say something, people listen. Soon the newspapers began to call him up, asking for his comments. A woman from a group called Urban Alliance on Race Relations came to interview him and she invited him to give a talk on the subject of discrimination in Canadian advertising. Oscar's message was simple and direct: Canadians should wake up and start showing greater tolerance for one another.

Roy McMurtry, the attorney general of Ontario at that time, suggested to Oscar that the two of them sit down with the heads of the companies that made the commercials, to try to persuade them to make some changes. Oscar agreed, and soon he found himself attending a series of luncheons with the bigshots of Canadian advertising. Oscar did not mince his words. He told the executives exactly how he felt about the discrimination he saw on television and in magazines.

The response to these meetings was mixed. Oscar said that some people seemed truly interested in making things better, while others did not see anything wrong with things as they were.

But even if Oscar and others failed to get everyone on side, their efforts produced some results. Over time, more minorities began to appear in commercials that aired on Canadian television, and in advertisements in Canadian magazines. Oscar never said much about the role he played in all of this, but others were more than willing to give him the credit he deserved. John Foss, president of the Association of Canadian Advertisers at that time, said that Oscar Peterson played an important part in making the advertising world aware of the discrimination that existed. In his opinion, "the industry largely corrected what was a terrible imbalance."

In 1988, Oscar admitted that he had started to see some changes, but he knew that any real change would take time. It would take more than just showing people how things were to get them to learn new values and greater respect for one another.

Oscar had spoken out and made people aware of an injustice that was taking place right under their noses. But he knew he was not a politician, or even an activist. He was first and foremost a musician, and even though he was getting older, he still had a lot of music left in him.

He continued to play with the various groups he had formed since his trio days with Ed Thigpen and Ray Brown. And as one of the great piano masters still working and recording, he had his pick of some of the finest rhythm section players around.

Then, in the mid-eighties, Ray Brown and Herb Ellis left their studio jobs. Over the next couple of years they were in touch with Oscar, and the three of them began to talk about the possibilities of a reunion.

Finally, in 1990, the first great Oscar Peterson Trio dusted off the cobwebs and picked up where it had left off thirty years earlier. By then Oscar, Ray and Herb were all well into their sixties. From the way they played, though, you could imagine they were kids again.

Duke Ellington (1899–1974)

Duke Edward Kennedy Ellington grew up in Washington, D.C., in an atmosphere of culture and refinement. His father had started out as a poor southern laborer and worked his way up to the position of butler for a wealthy Washington family. Ellington's mother came from a respected black middle-class family. From the time he was a small child, Duke Ellington was treated by his own family as someone special. He would stand outside his house and force his cousins to bow and curtsy to him, while he said, "I am the grand, noble, Duke; crowds will be running to me."

Ellington began to study piano when he was seven and showed a keen interest in ragtime. His father wanted him to become an artist, but Ellington turned down a scholarship in commercial art in order to pursue a career in music. In 1923 he moved to New York with a Washington band that formed the nucleus for the early Duke Ellington orchestra.

By 1927 the band had grown from five to twelve pieces and had taken up residence at the famous Cotton Club in Harlem. Over the next five years, Ellington and his orchestra climbed to the top of the jazz world, rivaled in popularity only by the great trumpeter, Louis Armstrong.

From early in his career, Duke Ellington showed a keen interest in composition and arranging. He had practically no formal knowledge in these areas, but he had great confidence in his own abilities and a vision of the orchestra he wanted to build. He taught himself harmony by working things out on the piano, and he learned how to arrange by trial and error. He would write out parts for his orchestra, and then he and the band would play through his arrangements and try out different possibilities.

This cooperative approach to composition was one of Ellington's greatest talents. Although he was a fine piano player, his orchestra was his real instrument. He came to have an intimate knowledge of each individual player's strengths and would highlight them in his writing.

Duke Ellington is regarded by many to be the most important composer in the history of jazz. Many of his pieces, some of them co-written with members of his band or with other arrangers (especially the brilliant Billy Strayhorn) quickly became jazz classics. In all, he wrote about two thousand compositions, including hundreds of short instrumental pieces and many longer works, including suites, film scores and sacred music.

One time Ellington was on a JATP tour with Oscar Peterson. The two of them were sitting backstage, and Ellington asked Oscar to play something for him. Oscar decided to play one of his favorite Ellington tunes, "Lady of the Lavender Mist." As Oscar played, Ellington came over to the piano with a puzzled expression on his face and asked Oscar what he was playing. "Duke," Oscar replied in astonishment, "that's one of your tunes." When Oscar had finished, Ellington explained that rather than dwelling on the past, he concentrated on what he was going to compose in the future.

Duke Ellington received many honors and awards over his long career, including the Presidential Medal of Honor in 1969.

11

Celebrating a Long Career

In 1991, Oscar Peterson was appointed chancellor — or honorary head — of York University in Toronto. He was deeply moved to be chosen for such a position. "Jazz people don't usually move in those circles," he said when he heard the news.

This appointment had special meaning for him. For all the fame and recognition he had achieved over his long career, he often felt that he was overlooked in his native country. At the official ceremony at York, he said these simple, touching words. "I've always wanted to feel wanted at home. I've always wanted to feel respected at home. I've always wanted to feel honored at home."

Oscar was sixty-six years old and closing in on his fiftieth year as a professional musician. And now he seemed to have found some peace in his personal life as well. In the early nineties he married his fourth wife, Kelly Green, who had been managing a restaurant in Florida when they met. A year after they were married, they had a daughter, Celine.

When he became chancellor at York, Oscar cut back even

more on his traveling and recording schedule. He seemed content to spend time at home, working on his composing. Besides, only a few clubs could afford to pay him the salary he now commanded. The Blue Note chain of clubs was one of them (one club in New York and three in Japan), and Oscar and his old buddies, Ray Brown and Herb Ellis, played there several times. It had been more than thirty years since they last played regularly as a trio, but from the moment they were reunited, they sounded as if they hadn't missed a day.

They recorded four live albums at the Blue Note, including *Saturday Night at the Blue Note*, which in 1991 received a Grammy for the Best Jazz Instrumental Performance by a Group. Oscar might have been slowing down, but he had no intention of retiring. He was inspired by the great musicians — including pianist Artur Rubinstein and conductor Arturo Toscanini — who continued to play and perform well into their old age. By this time, though, health problems were threatening to throw a crimp in his plans.

His arthritis was bothering him more, and he was suffering from the effects of being so overweight. He had begun to use a walker to give him more support, and in airports he needed a wheelchair. His friends and family were concerned. Oscar's father had died of a stroke, and they worried that Oscar might have one, too.

In May 1993, Oscar was playing at the Blue Note in New York. During a set, he turned to Ray Brown and said, "Look at my left hand... I can't use my left hand, it doesn't react." Incredible as it seems, Oscar kept playing, and he managed to finish the evening. Later he was examined by a doctor, who diagnosed a stroke. Oscar's whole left side, including his left hand, was badly damaged.

Years later, Oscar spoke about the period leading up to the

stroke: "I didn't know what was happening to me. I know I felt a little heady at times. I'd go up to my dressing room and things would sort of go in and out of focus for a moment... I just thought it was stress."

After his stroke, Oscar went through a very hard time, both physically and emotionally. His left hand — a hand that had been able to perform the most remarkable feats of speed and precision — now lay useless at his side. For a while he was so depressed that he could not summon the energy to care about anything anymore. "If that's the way it's going to end," he found himself thinking, "so that's the way it's going to end."

This was not the Oscar Peterson his family and friends had known over the years. And it was not the person the world had known, either — a man of incredible energy and determination, who had taken on one challenge after another, no matter how hard.

After some time, Oscar felt his old determination returning. Once he accepted what had happened to him, he focused all his energy on his recovery. He underwent intensive physiotherapy and refused to give in to the possibility that he might never perform again.

During this period, he turned more to his composing and playing his synthesizers. Slowly but surely, he felt himself getting stronger. Now it seemed only a matter of time before he would play in public, even if he could not use his left hand as he had before.

He started by playing for his young daughter's school class, just to test the waters. Things went well, and he began to make plans for a more official return. In order to make up for the loss of function in his left hand, he hired a guitarist for his band. The guitar would take care of most of the chording, and Oscar could concentrate on his right hand.

Only fourteen months after the stroke, Oscar performed at the Ravinia Festival near Chicago. He was now a jazz legend — one of the few players of his generation still playing — and his name alone could still draw large crowds. He sold out the 3,500-seat pavilion, and thousands more sat on the lawn.

His return was triumphant. He proved that audiences still loved to hear him, even if he could no longer play with quite the flash of his former days. But music is about far more than how many notes you can play. After his stroke, Oscar's ballad playing became warmer and deeper. It was as if his physical limitations had given him more time to reflect on what he wanted to say in his playing. And as many people have observed, Oscar Peterson still plays better with one hand than many pianists do with two.

Throughout the 1990s, he continued to receive honors and awards. In 1997, he received a Grammy Lifetime Achievement Award, his eighth Grammy to that point. In August 1999, the auditorium at Montreal's Concordia University was renamed the Oscar Peterson Concert Hall. Later that same year, he was awarded the prestigious Praemium World Art Award by the Japan Art Association. Over the years he received numerous honorary degrees — fifteen through 1999. New honors come his way so often that any list of them is soon out of date, but the Internet is a good way to keep up with more recent ones.

Perhaps the most significant award of all, though, was the one he received in 1984 from his own country, when he was invested as a Companion of the Order of Canada, the highest honor that can be bestowed on a Canadian citizen. The citation he was given at the award ceremony read, "With his classical bent and passion for perfection, Oscar Peterson is probably today's finest jazz pianist. By virtue of his many world tours, he has become Canada's musical ambassador. He is a staunch champion of the equality of our ethnic minorities."

★ ★ ★

Oscar Peterson was not an innovator, nor did he ever claim to be one. He did not create a new approach to playing jazz piano, as did Earl Hines or Thelonious Monk or Cecil Taylor. What he did do, as well as or better than any player of his time, was to study and absorb the work of the master musicians who came before him, as well as that of his contemporaries. He took his great knowledge and used it to make his own statement. The results have been spectacular.

Individuality is highly prized in jazz. Musicians try to develop their own ways of expressing their musical ideas, rather than simply copying another player. The many jazz pianists who have admired Oscar Peterson are not necessarily trying to play like him. Most of them would admit that they would not be able to even if they wanted. Also, while most players today are interested in playing in a more contemporary style, Oscar has never strayed far from the swinging, bluesy jazz he has played since the late 1940s.

Nonetheless, he has earned the respect and even awe of many of his peers. Herbie Hancock, one of the finest jazz pianists of the past forty years, once said that Oscar is "probably the greatest living influence in jazz piano today." Hancock meant that all jazz pianists who came after Oscar took him into account, even if they played in a very different way. He and Oscar became good friends, and in the early eighties they even performed as a duo.

For his part, Oscar has always listened carefully to other pianists and he expressed great admiration for Bill Evans, Hank Jones and Phineas Newborn, Jr. Later on he offered guidance and support to Monty Alexander, a Jamaican-born pianist whose virtuosic brilliance is similar to Oscar's. In the nineties, Oscar befriended the young pianist Benny Green, and they made a recording together.

But for all his admirers, Oscar has also drawn criticism. Some people have accused him of selling out, of playing a more popular style of jazz in order to appeal to a wider audience. Others have said that his playing is cold and mechanical, that he relies too much on his technique in order to dazzle his listeners.

Oscar offers no apologies for the way he plays. He admits that sometimes Norman Granz asked his musicians to play in a simpler style for certain audiences, and Oscar did not mind doing that. He once said, "If you pick up a science book and you can't understand a word that's written in it, you can't say, 'That's a good book,' because you don't know what you're talking about. If you listen to a song and say, 'Wow, I like that,' then you understand something about that music."

These words sum up his philosophy about music as well as any. He has always believed that people go to hear music to have a good time, not to have to struggle to understand what the music is all about. He feels strongly that jazz music should have a strong melody and that it should swing, and both his playing and his compositions are proof of this belief.

He is proud of his brilliant technique, and he sees no reason why he should keep it under wraps. From the time he was a young child, it was clear that he had remarkable physical ability. Then, when he studied with Paul de Marky, he learned the two-handed, virtuosic style of the nineteenth century. Oscar excelled in this style, and it had a great influence on how he played jazz. His playing has not always been to everyone's taste, but part of being an artist is knowing that you can't please all the people all the time. Oscar has always enjoyed a large following of devoted fans, and that is all that really matters.

★ ★ ★

As Oscar reached his mid-seventies, he experienced the loss of some of his closest friends and family. Norman Granz's death from cancer in 2001 left Oscar "both personally bereaved and creatively drained." In 2002, Ray Brown died in his sleep while on tour. And in the same year, Oscar's second-oldest daughter, Sharon, died of kidney disease.

Despite these losses, Oscar continued to play. In 2002, he was the featured artist at a performance before Queen Elizabeth II, on the occasion of her Golden Jubilee. Afterward, as the Queen came on stage to meet the performers, the camera paused on Oscar's smiling face, his twelve-year-old daughter, Celine, standing proudly at his side.

★ ★ ★

Oscar Peterson's roots were modest. He was the son of Caribbean immigrants who worked hard to build a life for themselves and their five children in their new country. He was part of the small black population in a mainly white, mainly French-speaking city. He was a minority within a minority.

He might have looked different from many of the children he went to school with, but he learned at a young age that people were simply people. There were good people and bad people of all shades and colors. And as proud as he was of his black heritage, he always thought of himself "first and foremost as a human being."

As a child he experienced what it felt like to be called names because he was black. Later, when he became a professional musician, he noticed that even at a time of segregation and discrimination against blacks and other minorities, musicians of all colors played and socialized together.

That was the kind of world Oscar Peterson wanted to live in — a world where people were treated with dignity and respect. "I guess it means we're going to have to turn the world into a world of performers," Oscar once said, "so they understand what love is all about."

GLOSSARY

bebop: The jazz style that came to prominence in the 1940s, featuring twisting, complicated melody lines and chord changes.

blues: A musical form, usually twelve or sixteen bars in length, common in jazz and other popular music.

boogie-woogie: A piano style popular in the 1930s, featuring a repetitive bass figure in the left hand and a strong eighth-note swing feel.

Dixieland: A jazz style popular in the 1910s and 1920s featuring two beats to the bar and collective improvisation.

dynamics: The range of volume at which a piece of music is played.

gig: Any performance for which a musician is paid.

harmony: The chords that accompany a melody.

head: A term used by jazz musicians to refer to the melody or theme of a piece of music.

improvisation: The creation of melodies, harmonies or rhythms that deviate in some way from the original form. Improvisation is one of the most important features of jazz music.

jam session: An informal musical gathering, often without an audience, in which musicians can try out new ideas and work on improvising without the constraints of formal performance.

JATP (Jazz at the Philharmonic): The integrated company of musicians founded by promoter Norman Granz in the mid-1940s and active through the 1960s. JATP toured around the world and brought jazz greater popularity and respect while breaking down racial barriers.

Jim Crow: The system of segregation named after a black minstrel character in a song from the 1830s. Jim Crow laws enforced two standards for blacks and whites in education, public places and social customs.

jukebox: A machine that plays a selection of recorded music when a coin is inserted.

notation: The representation of pitches and rhythms using symbols on a musical staff.

perfect pitch: The ability to identify notes just by hearing them.

ragtime: A style of piano playing popular in the late nineteenth and early twentieth centuries, featuring a syncopated melody in the right hand over a steady accompaniment in the left hand.

riff: A repeated figure, often played by the brass and saxophone sections as background for the soloist.

scat: A style of jazz vocalizing in which made-up syllables are used instead of words.

side: A three-minute recording that fit onto one side of a two-sided disc called a 78.

sitting in: The term used when a musician is invited on stage to perform with the band.

solo: The part of a jazz performance when one musician improvises.

stride: A piano style of the 1920s (made popular by Jelly Roll Morton and James P. Johnson) that kept a steady pulse in the left hand while the right hand performed swift, tricky lines up and down the piano.

swing: The style of jazz that flourished from 1935 to 1945, employing thousands of musicians in big bands across the U.S. The swing style combined sweet dance music with hotter "swing" numbers. The most famous swing bands included those of Duke Ellington, Count Basie, Benny Goodman and Glenn Miller.

swung eighth notes: The style of playing eighth notes where the note landing on the "down" or strong beat is played slightly longer than the note on the "up" beat. As jazz has evolved, this "swing" feel has changed and been expressed in different ways.

synthesizer: An electronic instrument that can make a wide range of sounds, including those of many other musical instruments.

territory bands: Touring bands that played through the mid- and southwestern United States in the 1920s and 1930s.

voicings: The particular arrangement of notes in a chord.

FURTHER READING

Coker, Jerry. *Listening to Jazz*. (Prentice-Hall, 1978). An excellent guide to understanding jazz improvisation and theory, as well as the roles of the various instruments in a jazz ensemble, with a brief look at the major jazz styles and the key contributors to each style.

Collier, James Lincoln. *Jazz: An American Saga*. (Henry Holt, 1997). An examination of the history of jazz in America, from its roots in African music, gospel and blues, and on through swing, bebop and free jazz. Short studies with wonderful photographs of some of the innovators from each period.

Collier, James Lincoln. *The Great Jazz Artists*. (Four Winds Press/Scholastic, 1977). Short biographies of several well-known jazz musicians, including Scott Joplin, Bessie Smith, Duke Ellington, Django Reinhardt, Charlie Parker and John Coltrane.

Collier, James Lincoln. *Louis Armstrong: An American Success Story*. (MacMillan, 1985). An excellent biography of Louis Armstrong, the brilliant New Orleans trumpeter, one of the most important and influential jazz musicians of the twentieth century.

Frankl, Ron. *Duke Ellington: Bandleader and Composer*. (Chelsea House/Main Line, 1988). This book is from a series called Black Americans of Achievement and looks at Ellington's achievements as bandleader and composer. Excellent photographs of Ellington, his family and his orchestra, as well as other key musicians of the era.

Frankl, Ron. *Miles Davis*. (Chelsea House, 1996). The story of one of the most influential trumpeters in the history of jazz.

Gourse, Leslie. *Billie Holiday: The Tragedy and Triumph of Lady Day*. (Franklin Watts/Grolier, 1995). The story of the legendary jazz singer who sang with an honesty and passion that moves listeners to this day. Gourse chronicles Holiday's lifelong battle with drug and alcohol addiction, racism and unhappy personal relationships.

Gourse, Leslie. *Blowing on the Changes: The Art of the Jazz Horn Players*. (Franklin Watts/Grolier, 1997). Gourse looks at some of the jazz world's most renowned brass and reed players, from Louis Armstrong, Lester Young and Dizzy Gillespie to the leading figures of recent years, including Wynton Marsalis, Roy Hargrove and Vincent Herring.

Gourse, Leslie. *Dizzy Gillespie and the Birth of Bebop* (Atheneum, 1994). A biography of one of the most influential musicians of the bebop era.

Hentoff, Nat. *Does This School Have Capital Punishment?* (Delacorte, 1981). Young Sam Davidson befriends an older jazz musician, who helps him out when he is falsely accused of having marijuana in his possession at school.

Newton, Suzanne. *I Will Call It Georgie's Blues* (Viking, 1983). Neal Sloan, the fifteen-year-old son of a strict Baptist minister, keeps his love of jazz piano a secret, until a family crisis leads him to reveal his true self.

Shapiro, Nat and Hentoff, Nat, eds. *Hear Me Talkin' to Ya: The Story of Jazz as Told by the Men Who Made It.* (Dover, 1955). Interviews with many of the key figures (men and women!) from the early days of jazz up to the mid-1950s. One of the classic books of jazz history.

Juan Williams, *Eyes on the Prize: America's Civil Rights Years, 1954–1965.* (Viking Penguin, 1987), pp. 10, 12–13. "A Companion Volume to the PBS Television Series." An excellent account of the struggle for civil rights in America, with stunning photographs of some of the major figures and events that shaped the movement.

VIDEOS

In the Key of Oscar. Elitha Peterson Productions Inc./Vocal Vision Productions Inc, 1992, in association with the National Film Board of Canada and the Canadian Broadcasting Corporation. A moving and revealing portrait of Oscar Peterson and his family as they gather for a reunion. Interviews with many of the key figures in Peterson's life, including his sister Daisy and several of his children, as well as musicians Ray Brown, Herb Ellis, Ella Fitzgerald and Peterson's longtime friend and manager, Norman Granz.

Nat King Cole: Unforgettable. An MPI Home Entertainment Release. MP 1663. Copyright 1989 EMI Records. The life of the outstanding singer and pianist whose work influenced many jazz musicians, including Oscar Peterson. (Peterson is interviewed in the film.)

Jazz. A Film by Ken Burns. Produced by Ken Burns and Lynn Novick, 2000. A ten-part documentary that looks at jazz from a social and historical perspective and includes an in-depth study of the music itself. Beautifully photographed, with wonderful footage of the people and places at the center of jazz.

WEBSITES

http://www.oscarpeterson.com/
Peterson's official website, which includes a Multimedia CD-ROM, Career Highlights, Awards and Honors, Music Samples and Transcriptions. Peterson himself contributes regular journal entries, sharing his thoughts about music, family and other musicians.

http://www.nlc-bnc.ca/oscarpeterson/m3-2044-e.html
An excellent exhibition of Peterson's life and career, with links to biographical information, a photo gallery, honors and recordings, including selections from some of his albums.

http://www.allaboutjazz.com/timeline.htm
Year-by-year timeline with brief description of the most important jazz events for that year, including recordings and concerts by the major figures.

http://www.jazzphotos.com
This website has hundreds of photos of jazz musicians, as well as a good list of links to other sites.

http://www.pbs.org/jazz/kids/
Some of this site is aimed at younger children, with interactive displays that allow the participant to repeat phrases and rhythms. However, there is a timeline for older kids, with interesting photographs and text placing the time and place in a jazz context.

LISTENING GUIDE

Oscar Peterson is certainly one of the most recorded jazz musicians of all time; in a recent search I found almost 200 CDs currently available. This list is therefore only intended as a preliminary guide to some of his better known recordings, or to those that illustrate a particular aspect of his playing, such as his trio and solo work or his recordings as accompanist.

1. *Beginnings, 1945–1949*. BMG
A 2-CD set of Oscar Peterson with his trio and quartet in his earliest recordings. Recorded in Montreal 1945–1949. Oscar's technical brilliance is obvious, but he is still focused on boogie-woogie and is a few years away from reaching his mature style.

2. *Oscar Peterson: The Song is You. Best of the Verve Songbooks*. Verve: PolyGram. Original recordings produced by Norman Granz from 1952 to 1959.
This 2-CD collection is a good introduction to the "songbook" albums produced by Norman Granz in the 1950s, albums based on the work of one composer, such as Cole Porter or George Gershwin, etc. It includes sessions of Oscar Peterson with Herb Ellis, Ray Brown, Barney Kessel and Ed Thigpen in various trio combinations.

3. *Stan Getz and the Oscar Peterson Trio*. Verve.
On this 1958 album Oscar Peterson, Herb Ellis and Ray Brown accompany the great tenor saxophonist, Stan Getz — one of the many albums the trio made in the 1950s with the outstanding soloists of the day.

4. *Ella and Louis* (1956) and *Ella and Louis Again* (1957). Verve.
More of Oscar, Ray and Herb in the role of accompanists, along with Buddy Rich and Louis Bellson on drums. Ella Fitzgerald and Louis

Armstrong sing beautifully together, and Louis also plays trumpet on these sessions that include some classic jazz standards.

5. *The Oscar Peterson Trio at the Stratford Shakespearean Festival.* Verve: PolyGram. Original recording produced by Norman Granz. Recorded in concert at the Stratford Shakespearean Festival in Ontario, Canada, August 8, 1956, this is one of Oscar's classic recordings with Ray Brown and Herb Ellis.

6. *The Oscar Peterson Trio: Canadiana Suite.* Polygram.
The *Canadiana Suite* (recorded in 1964) is Oscar Peterson's first extended composition, a collection of connected pieces — a suite — that he wrote as a tribute to Canada. He has recorded individual pieces from the suite, including "Place St. Henri," "Wheatland," and "March Past" on several later recordings.

7. *Oscar Peterson: Exclusively for My Friends. The lost tapes.* Verve Records.
This is a collection from Oscar Peterson's MPS albums that he recorded in Germany between 1963 and 1968 with recording engineer Hans Georg Brunner-Schwer. It features Oscar's trios of that era and includes originals and jazz standards. With Ray Brown (bass), Bobby Durham (drums), Sam Jones (bass), and Ed Thigpen (drums).

8. *The London House Sessions. Oscar Peterson Trio.* Verve: Polygram.
This is a 5-CD collection of Oscar Peterson with Ray Brown and Ed Thigpen, recorded live at the London House, Chicago, in the summer of 1961.

9. *Night Train.* Verve: PolyGram. One of Oscar's best-selling albums, *Night Train* was also highly praised by the critics. Recorded in 1962 with Ray Brown and Ed Thigpen, the album shows the trio's intense, swinging feel.

10. *History of an Artist.* Pablo. (2-CD collection)
In the early 1970s, Oscar Peterson and Norman Granz had the idea to

make a collection of recordings that would recreate Oscar's career by bringing into the studio musicians from his various bands to that point. There are selections of Oscar on solo piano, duo recordings with Ray Brown and tracks with various guitar and drum trios.

11. *If You Could See Me Now. The Oscar Peterson Four*. Pablo.
The brilliant guitarist Joe Pass played with Oscar Peterson for many years. This is a 1983 recording of the Oscar Peterson quartet with Oscar, Joe Pass, bassist Niels-Henning Ørsted Pedersen and drummer Martin Drew.

12. *The Legendary Oscar Peterson Trio Live at the Blue Note*. Telarc. Recorded in New York City, March, 1990. Oscar, Ray and Herb began playing together after a separation of twenty years and made several recordings, including this one with Bobby Durham on drums.

13. *Oscar Peterson: A Summer Night in Munich*. Telarc, 1999. This recent album features Oscar with his most recent quartet of Ulf Wakenius (guitar), Niels-Henning Ørsted Pedersen (bass), and Martin Drew (drums). Oscar has once again found bandmates who can match his virtuosity.

14. *Trail of Dreams: a Canadiana Suite*. Telarc, 2000.
Composed by Oscar Peterson and arranged by Michel Legrand. This is another extended composition Oscar Peterson wrote with a Canadian theme. With the same musicians as listed in number 13, and also The Michel Legrand Strings.

NOTES

p. 11, "I'll bet one..." Gene Lees, *Oscar Peterson: The Will to Swing* (Toronto: Key Porter Books, 2000), p. 32.

p. 12, "You apologize..." Ibid.

p. 15, Discussion of childhood mortality and public health in Montreal, T. Copp, *The Anatomy of Poverty: The Condition of the Working Class in Montreal, 1897–1929* (Toronto: McClelland and Stewart Ltd., 1974) as told in D.W. Williams, *The Road to Now: A History of Blacks in Montreal* (Montreal:Vehicule Press, 1988), p. 51.

p. 16, "any other Negro..." Oscar Peterson in *In the Key of Oscar*. Elitha Peterson Productions Inc./Vocal Vision Productions Inc. in association with the National Film Board of Canada and the Canadian Broadcasting Corporation.

p. 19, "He didn't have..." Daisy Peterson as quoted in Lees, p. 16. "The teacher came..." Ibid.

p. 20, "Music was the..." Barbara Cooper, interview with Dorothy W. Williams, July 12, 1995, as quoted in *The Road to Now*, p. 76.

"must have had..." Daisy Peterson Sweeney in *In the Key of Oscar*.

Oscar Peterson's discussion of Daisy's teaching: From CBC-TV, Oscar Peterson portrait, 2/83, as quoted in Lees, p. 26.

p. 23, "What did you..." Oscar Peterson in *In the Key of Oscar*. "Fine, now here's..." Lees, p. 33.

p. 27, "looking very neat..." and "He knew them..." Lou Hooper, *That Happy Road* (unpublished autobiography), National Archives of Canada. As quoted in Lees, pp. 36–37.

p. 28, "As the door..." Oscar Peterson, *A Jazz Odyssey: The Life of Oscar Peterson* (London: Continuum, 2002), p. 46.

"No, No! That's..." Peterson, p. 47.

pp. 28-29, "Paul de Marky..." Lees, p. 37.

p. 29, "speedy fingers, because..." Lees, p. 38.

pp. 34-35, Discussion of boogie-woogie from James Lincoln Collier, *The Great Jazz Artists* (New York.: Four Winds Press, 1977), p. 82.

p. 35, Discussion of stride from James Lincoln Collier, *Jazz: An American Saga* (New York, Henry Holt and Company, Inc., 1997), p. 25.

p. 36, "I'll never forget..." "Oscar Peterson In Conversation With André Previn." An illustrated musical reminiscence broadcast on Omnibus, BBC-TV, 11/12/74, as quoted in Richard Palmer, *Oscar Peterson*. (Kent: Spellmount Ltd., 1984), p. 16.

p. 37, "Some day I'm..." Hal Gaylor as told to Gene Lees in Lees, p. 41.

p. 38, Discussion of Marcus Garvey, *In the Key of Oscar*; also Williams, pp. 58–59.

p. 39, "There are a..." *In the Key of Oscar*.

p. 41, Art Tatum Biography. See Collier, *The Great Jazz Artists*, pp. 88–89.

p. 44, "First of all..." Lees, p. 42.

p. 45, "Okay, kid, go..." Ibid.

p. 46, "You got it," Mark Miller, *Such Melodious Racket: The Lost History of Jazz in Canada, 1914–1949* (Toronto: The Mercury Press, 1997), p. 250.

"He already had..." John Gilmore, *Swinging in Paradise: The Story of Jazz in Montreal* (Montreal: Véhicule Press, 1988), p. 100.

p. 47, "He got it..." Ibid, p. 101.

"a diamond in..." Lees, p. 45.

p. 48, "[Johnny Holmes] is..." Quoted in Harold Dingman, "Oscar Peterson," *Liberty* (12 January 1946), p. 19, as quoted in Miller, *Such Melodious Racket*, p. 253.

p. 49, Story of Peterson at the Ritz-Carlton. See Lees, p. 51; Miller, *Such Melodious Racket*, p. 253.

p. 50, "I just fell..." Lees, p. 47.

"Certainly, his wonderful..." "How He Proposed, by Mrs. Oscar Peterson," *Tan Romances* (September 1953), as quoted in Lees, p. 48.

"So, let's you..." Ibid.

p. 52, "had some clout." Oscar Peterson in *In the Key of Oscar*.

Count Basie's reaction to hearing Oscar Peterson from Herb Johnson, "Montreal doings," *Music Dial* (August 1944), p. 15, as told in

Miller, *Such Melodious Racket*, p. 253.

p. 53, "fire and finesse." *Jazz-Hot* (April 1973), as quoted in Gérald Arnaud and Jacques Chesnel, *Masters of Jazz* (W & R Chambers Ltd., 1991), p 40.

"That's it. That's…" Meet-the-Stars, as told in Lees, p. 306.

p. 55, Nat Cole biography. See Barry Kernfeld, ed., *The New Grove Dictionary of Jazz* (New York: Grove's Dictionaries Inc., 2002),. Nat Cole entry; also, Leslie Gourse, *Unforgettable: The Life and Mystique of Nat King Cole* (New York: St. Martin's Press, 1991), pp. 182–186.

p. 57, "Call up a…" Dingman, *Liberty*, p. 19, as told in Gilmore, p. 106.

p. 59, "My first two…" "Man! That Re-bop's hep, boogie passe," Vancouver *Sun* (7 October 1946), p. 5, as told in Miller, *Such Melodious Racket*, p. 256.

Racist incident with cab. See Lees, p. 50.

p. 60, "We just let…" John Gilmore. *Swinging in Paradise*, p. 105.

p. 62, "Do you really…" As reported by Lou Hooper, Jr. to John Gilmore in *Swinging in Paradise*, p. 108.

p. 64, "a great pianist." CBC-TV, as cited in Lees, p. 26.

p. 65, "I love your…" As told by Oscar Peterson in *In the Key of Oscar*; also in *A Jazz Odyssey*, p. 107.

p. 66, Count Basie biography. "take care of…" *Good Morning Blues: The Autobiography of Count Basie*, as told to Albert Murray. (New York: Random House, 1985), p. xi.

"COUNT BASIE. Beware…" Ibid, p. 17.

p. 67, "an idol and…" Peterson, p. 283.

"I just sit…" Basie, p. 366.

p. 72, Story of Norman Granz meeting Oscar Peterson. In Leonard Feather, *From Satchmo to Miles* (New York: Stein and Day, 1972), p. 190, as told in Gilmore, p. 109; Lees, p. 63.

p. 73, "Take your best…" Lees, p. 64.

p. 74, "a rhythmic punch…" Quoted in *Down Beat* (October 21, 1949), as quoted in Lees, pp. 69–70.

"He burst upon…" Richard Palmer, *Oscar Peterson* (Kent: Spellmount Ltd., 1984), p. 15.

p. 77, "Travelling in the..." June Callwood, "The Oscar Petersons," *Maclean's* (September 25, 1958), as quoted in Lees, p. 103.

"They're not planning..." Oscar Peterson in *In the Key of Oscar*.

Discussion of Jim Crow. See Juan Williams, *Eyes on the Prize: America's Civil Rights Years, 1954–1965* (New York: Viking Penguin Inc., 1987), pp. 10, 12–13.

p. 78, Story of Ella Fitzgerald and Southern cop. As told by Oscar Peterson in *In the Key of Oscar*.

p. 79, "Where did you..." and "Pick it up..." From story told by Oscar Peterson to Audrey Morris and Stuart Genovese, as told in Lees, p. 103.

p. 82, Ben Webster on Oscar Peterson's practice routine with Ray Brown, from Steve Voce, "It Don't Mean A Thing," *Jazz Journal* (3/67), p. 24, as quoted in Palmer, p. 23.

p. 82, "Is this possible..." Lees, p. 136.

"Ray has an..." Lees, p. 139.

p. 84, "Mr. McQuaid did..." Lees, p. 86.

p. 86, Ray Brown biography. See Lees, pp. 137–140 and *The New Grove Dictionary of Jazz*, Ray Brown entry.

p. 88, "close-knit unit." Oscar Peterson in *In the Key of Oscar*.

p. 89, "If you want..." Leonard Feather, "The New Life of Ray Brown," *Down Beat* (9 March 1967), p. 25, as quoted in Palmer, p. 23.

"three people that..." "Oscar Peterson: The Compleat Pianist." An illustrated conversation conducted by Peter Clayton and broadcast on BBC Radio 3 on 12 April, 1974, as quoted in Palmer, p. 22.

p. 90, "the lock-down going," Lees, p. 128.

p. 91, "He's never come..." *Time* magazine (1951) private, unpublished internal office memorandum with *Time* researcher, as quoted in Lees, p. 92.

"Well, he's escaped..." Oscar Peterson in *In the Key of Oscar*.

"wipe every piano..."

"You understand, they..." Lees, p. 109.

"Just what do..." Lees, p. 111.

p. 97, "I don't want..." Lees, p. 132.

p. 98, "The greatest living..." "Swing, with Harmonics," *Time*,

(12/28/53), as quoted in Lees, p. 98.

"I was totally..." Len Lyons. *The Great Jazz Pianists: Speaking of Their Lives and Music.* (reprint, Cambridge: Da Capo, 1989), p. 135.

Story of Oscar Peterson and Art Tatum. See Lees, p. 102.

p. 99, "In one week..." Lyons, p. 136.

"I know I..." and "I still think..." From November 6, 1999 videotape of 17th Annual Floating Jazz Festival Meet-the-Stars event, as quoted in Lees, p. 307.

p. 101, Herb Ellis biography. Lees, p. 106; *The New Grove Dictionary of Jazz*, Herb Ellis entry.

p. 102, "I couldn't find..." Herb Ellis in *In the Key of Oscar.*

p. 103, Story about discrimination in Oscar Peterson's new neighborhood in Toronto. Lees, pp. 155–156.

p. 105, "Well, y'never know..." Ed Thigpen as quoted in Lees, p. 143.

p. 106, "steaming zone." Peterson, p. 221.

p. 107, "Okay, it's here..." and "six years of..." Lees, p. 151.

"The interesting thing..." Steve Voce, "It Don't Mean A Thing," *Jazz Journal* (2/71), p. 28, as quoted in Palmer, p. 53.

p. 108, Ben Webster on Oscar Peterson as accompanist. *Voce* (3/67), p. 24, as quoted in Palmer, p. 52.

"makes you want..." Ella Fitzgerald in *In the Key of Oscar.*

p. 110, "What was that..." Lees, p. 154.

p. 111, "Describe the background..." Ibid.

p. 112, Oscar on playing in basement with Ed and Ray. Lees, p. 162.

p. 114, "Frankly, at that..." Leonard Feather, "The New Life of Ray Brown," *Down Beat* (4/9/67), as quoted in Lees, p. 196.

p. 115, "I could never..." Leonard Feather, *Satchmo to Miles* (Quartet, 1974), p. 194, as quoted in Palmer, p. 13.

p. 116, Ella Fitzgerald biography. See *Jazz*, A Film by Ken Burns. Part 6. Jazz Swing: The Velocity of Celebration (1937-1939), produced by Ken Burns, Lynn Novick; also, *The New Grove Dictionary of Jazz*, Ella Fitzgerald entry.

p. 120, "Perhaps it was..." François Postif, "Oscar Peterson," *Jazz Hot* (9/69), as quoted in Lees, p. 210.

p. 121, "In a group..." Previn, as quoted in Palmer, p. 44.

p. 126, "a dreadful loss." Peterson, p. 361.

"That's the beautiful…" Mark Miller. *Boogie, Pete and the Senator. Canadian Musicians in Jazz: The Eighties* (Toronto: Nightwood Editions, 1987), p. 218.

pp. 126–127, Story of Oscar raking leaves with his son. Told by Oscar Peterson to Audrey Morris and Stuart Genovese, as quoted in Lees, p. 280.

p. 127, "we're all human…" Gene Lees, "All That Oscar," *Toronto Life* (9/81), as told in Lees, p. 230.

p.128, "It was a…" Ibid.

p. 129, "the industry largely…" Lees, p. 234.

pp. 130, Ellington biography. "I am the…" James Lincoln Collier, *Duke Ellington: The Life and Times of the Restless Genius of Jazz.* (London: Pan Books, 1989), p. 12; *The New Grove Dictionary of Jazz*, Duke Ellington entry.

p. 131, "Duke, that's one…" Peterson, p. 263.

p. 132, "Jazz people don't…" Lees, p. 286.

"I've always wanted…" From Oscar Peterson's speech at installation ceremony. From *In the Key of Oscar*.

p. 133, "Look at my…" Lees, p. 289.

p. 134, "I didn't know…" Interview with Billy Taylor for CBS Sunday Morning Show, 1998, as quoted in Lees, p. 289.

"If that's the…" Ibid.

p. 136, "probably the greatest…" Herbie Hancock in *In the Key of Oscar*.

p. 137, "If you pick…" *Now* magazine, June, 1991, as quoted in Lees, p. 287.

p. 138, "both personally bereaved…" Peterson, Prefatory Note.

"first and foremost…" Mike Hennessey, "An Interview with Oscar Peterson," *Gallery* (6/76), p. 40, as quoted in Palmer, p. 58.

p. 139, "I guess it…" Oscar Peterson in *In the Key of Oscar*.

"My father had…" Lees, p. 262.

ACKNOWLEDGMENTS

I would like to acknowledge my debt to the following writers, whose work I relied upon heavily in the preparation of my manuscript.

Gene Lees, for his biography, *Oscar Peterson: The Will to Swing*; Mark Miller, for his writing on jazz and Canadian jazz history in particular, especially his books *Such Melodious Racket: The Lost History of Jazz in Canada*, and *Boogie, Pete and the Senator: Canadian Musicians in Jazz: The Eighties*; John Gilmore, for *Swinging in Paradise: The Story of Jazz in Montreal;* Dorothy W. Williams, for *The Road to Now: A History of Blacks in Montreal*; Richard Palmer, for his discographical biography, *Oscar Peterson*; and of course Oscar Peterson himself, for his recently published autobiography, *A Jazz Odyssey: The Life of Oscar Peterson*. Also James Lincoln Collier, for his excellent books of jazz history and biography for adults and children.

Thanks to the following people who assisted me in my search for photographs and the permissions for their use: Lynda Barnett, CBC Design Library and Still Photo Collection; Nathalie Hodgson, Concordia University Archives, Montreal; Robert Kennell, Canadian Pacific Railway; Maureen Nevins, Music Division, National Library of Canada; Erika Savage, Universal Music; Julie Kirsh and Jillian Goddard, Sun Media Corporation; and Glenda Williams, City of Toronto Archives.

I would like to thank everyone at Groundwood, especially Nan Froman for her kindness and support; Michael Solomon for his masterful art direction; and Shelley Tanaka for her wonderful editing of the manuscript.

INDEX

St. Antoine, 15-16, 31, 39, 45-46, 49, 104

St. Croix, 13

St. Henri, 12, 15-16, 20, 30-31

St. Kitts, 14-15

stock arrangements, 47

"Straighten Up and Fly Right," 55

Stratford Shakespearean Festival, Ontario, 95

Strayhorn, Billy, 131

stride, 34-35, 58, 66-67, 141

Sweeney, Daisy. *See* Peterson, Daisy.

swing, 34, 58, 66-67, 141

swung eighth notes, 33, 141

synthesizer, 122 124, 141

Tatum, Art, 32, 35-36, 39, 41-42, 58, 98-100

Taylor, Cecil, 136

"Tenderly," 74

territory bands, 86, 101, 141

The Corner, 39, 44-45, 62

"The Happy Gang," 31

The Merchant Navy Show, 51

The Way I Really Play, 120

Thigpen, Ben, 104

Thigpen, Ed, 104-7, 109-10, 112, 114, 118, 121, 123-124, 129

Thoman, Stefan, 28

Thomas, William, 24

"Tiger Rag," 25

Time, 98

Toledo, Ohio, 41

Tophatters, 53

Toronto, 30, 60, 103, 114, 123

Toronto Life, 127

Toscanini, Arturo, 133

Tracks, 120

Trouville Club, 69

Twelve Royal Dukes, 55

"Undecided," 117

Union United Church, 17, 20, 38, 50

Urban Alliance on Race Relations, 128

Vancouver *Sun*, 58

Verdun, 49, 53

Verve, 95, 111

Victoria, 71-72

Victoria Hall, 47

Villingen, 118-19

voicings, 34, 43, 105, 141

Wade, Harold (Steep), 44-46, 48, 53, 62

Waller, Thomas (Fats), 32, 41, 66

Walton, Cedar, 86

Washington, D.C., 98, 130

Watanabe, Jiro (Butch), 31-32, 109

Webb, Chick, 37, 117

Webster, Ben, 76, 82

Westmount, 47

"What Is This Thing Called Love?" 61

Williams, Cootie, 105

Wilson, Teddy, 32, 53, 58, 80

Windsor Station. *See* Canadian Pacific Railway.

Winnipeg, 60

Wood Hall, 53

World War One, 13

World War Two, 51, 63, 68

Yonkers, 116

York University, 132

Young, Lee, 70

Young, Lester, 56, 67, 70, 76, 107